I0429973

Published by   : NYAMEAMA Publications
Printed by   : CreateSpace
Book Design by : Dennis Amoah Antwi
Edited by   : Wendy Linda Osei Akoto
Cover Design   : Ernest Nkrumah Taylor

ISBN-10 : 1500902586
ISBN-13 : 978-1500902582

AVAILABLE FROM:

Amazon and Other Online / Book Stores
And on Kindle and Other devices.

email: arnoldboateng@gmail.com

'There should be an African Dream;

A Dream of Societies of Opportunities,

Where the youth would be physically, mentally and spiritually equipped

To create Wealth, Grow their societies

And sustain the Societies for future Generations.

A Dream of a Continent where you can become whatever you aspire to be,

As long as you have the Skills and Ambition

Africa should be a Mother providing a home, education, job, food, and protection for all her Youth for them to secure fulfilment in their lives and acquire happiness'

Culled from:

'The African Youth Question'

TABLE OF CONTENT

BOOK ONE

CHAPTER 1

CHAPTER 2

CHAPTER 3

CHAPTER 4

CHAPTER 5

CHAPTER 6

CHAPTER 7

CHAPTER 8

CHAPTER 9

CHAPTER 10

CHAPTER 11

CHAPTER 12

THE CAREER SPECTRUM   116-120

BOOK TWO

DREAMS

CHAPTER 13

CHAPTER 14

THE END

Africa, Dream Again
Africa, Dream Beyond the Stars

DEDICATION

To the African Youth; Allim Musah Adoleba Atikese, BSc Administration, University of Ibadan, Nigeria; Unemployed;

Gyau Akapko Amiri, Dog Chain Seller, Kaneshie Traffic Light, Accra; Ghana;

Asibi Senam Amne; Fifteen (15) year old pregnant Kayayo, Rawlings Park, Accra; Ghana

And Afaafa Leila; Teacher, Touba; Dakar, Senegal

To the African youth:

That she would grow into the new society; viable, resourceful and healthy;

A society able to meet her needs as she aspires and strives for the African dream;
A dream of Societies of equal opportunities, abundance and prosperity,
A society where you can become whatever you want to be;
A dream of Nations defined by Ideas and stabilised by Compassion,

Personal Freedoms, Honesty, Love, Hard Work, Fairness and Contentment;

And not by Material Wealth, Greed, Depravity, Hatred, Ethnicity or Colour;

And finally to the Memories of Kwame Nkrumah, Antha Diop, Patrice Lumumba, Father Nyerere A Tafawa Belawa, Mandela and Jomo Kenyatta and all the founding fathers, that their grand children would finally find the path to fulfilment and prosperity;

The Lands of Gold.

ACKNOWLEDGEMENT

To the LORD GOD ALMIGHTY for the strength, energy and favour I enjoyed throughout the preparation of this book. I also express my warmest appreciation to the Helpers He brought my way.

Special thanks go to the Youth in Africa, who through their innovative initiatives, have given me the hope that, a new and better Africa is being born; we have a Future.

To Sefa Gohoho; a Pan African Entrepreneur for her wits and bold suggestions;

To David Charway; for the cover design;

To Daniel Lamptey for proofreading the work;

To Ernest Taylor, Tarkoradi Polytechnic for the book design;

To the many persons who supported me in all manner of ways;

To all who participated in the prayer sessions for this work;

To Samuel Nsiah; my Personal Assistant;

To my long-standing friend Akwasi Owusu Afrifa-Mensa for his support

And to Ohene Djan for his valuable contributions;

To the Hon Opare-Ansah, Member of Parliament for Suhum, Ghana, and Member of the ECOWAS Parliament, who gave me office space during the last few months of this work;

To my Wife and Son for their support and encouragement;

To The MOST HIGH be Glory and Honour.

FOREWORD

The youthful stage is a time to have a bit of fun. It is also a time for taking important decisions, which could influence your life for good or bad. Some decisions are obvious to make, some not much so. Sometimes it is easy to identify if a decision is right or wrong. Sometimes it is not, until later on in life, when it may be too late.

The current environment is fraught with many opportunities for your dreams to be realised. This book is a timely wake-up call for you to rise up to build and live your dreams. *The Dreams of Our Youth* is a humble attempt with deep social insights for the youth, political leaders and the society.

A bright and prosperous future could be lost or secured through the decisions you make today. The future is now. *The Dreams of Our Youth* is suitable for students, political leadership at the college, community and national levels, policy makers, civil society, the clergy and young entrepreneurs. I would not leave out traditional authorities.

Most of you would like more out of life than you already have. Yet, not many of you are able to achieve what you set out to do, no matter how hard you try. This could be as a result of you either choosing the wrong route or being discouraged by parents, guardians or even by your peers or not having the requisite skills and ability.

Let me now point out some challenges that normally face the youth:

Fear of failure is the biggest obstacle to success. Fear is a negative force that paralyses. Most people don't succeed because they are afraid to fail. They are so afraid of failure that they don't even take the first step towards their ambition, least of all to try to do things differently.

The secret to success, however, beyond skills, right attitude and counsel, is for one not to stop trying because of failure. What most of you call failure, I call it *a setback*. The moment you stop trying, you are condemned to fail. Many a great man have succeeded because they have not given up after they had failed several times. Rather, they kept trying and learning till success was attained. Once one is convinced that a certain venture is right, then 'try, try, try,' again until success is achieved. This should be your mantra.

Let me caution against blind ambitions. You must train yourself to acquire the skills which are necessary to achieve your dreams. If you fail to master the required skills, you would not be able to achieve your dreams no matter how hard and many times you try. This advice goes to all of you in business, school, politics and any endeavour in life. Prepare yourself for the dream and be patient to learn. Do not hesitate to seek guidance.

The action and inaction of friends and the public sometimes discourage you from fully realizing your talents and dreams. This could be a big obstacle to success. Some are always ready to say 'it cannot be done'. Such people could be obstacles to achieving your dreams and career aspirations.

However, at times, such admonitions could be a caution to change course for the better. When confronted with such a situation, you need to evaluate your options and make a choice based on informed knowledge and conviction.

It is important for you to realize that success, defined as achieving one's dreams, is a long journey with many roadblocks.

It is the people who overcome the roadblocks who are regarded by society as successful.

It is said that, 'procrastination is the thief of time'. At no time is this more important in one's life than at the youthful stage. The habits of postponing decisions and actions, laziness, daydreaming and unproductive lifestyles (excessive drinking, drug addiction, pervasiveness and living beyond one's means) would, to a large extent, hinder you from reaching your lofty goals in life. Habits are addictive. Addictions have to be stopped stage by stage. After all, one does not acquire bad habits overnight.

Suffice to say, you must control your desires for pleasures, avoid drugs, alcohol and bad friendship. The youth should never play with their education, while in school and on the job, which is the only sure foundation for success in these times.

Life is a journey. It calls for knowledge, skills, humility, hard work, pursuit of excellence, respect for the law and, above all, commitment. I urge every young person to remember this.

It is my hope that this book will inspire you to think international and global. It would also guide you as to how to set achievable goals; get the right education; the paths to take; what to expect in its course and will encourage you to achieve your set dreams. Suffice to say, it is important for you to acquire the necessary network and capacity to be able to compete successfully in the global arena you dream of.

Political leadership has key roles to play in implementing youth policies which would meet your aspirations. Additionally, there is the need to see the youth as partners in development.

Kwaku Boateng says most of it all and addresses the need for one to realize their dreams in times such as this. *The Dreams of*

Our Youth is not only a must-read for every youth, it is a must-practice for every youth desiring to realise and live his destiny.

Good times are ahead for our Lands: Africa.

Stay blessed!

PRESIDENT JOHN AGYEKUM KUFUOR

President of the Republic of Ghana

January 9th, 2001 – January 8th, 2009

INTRODUCTION

First Thoughts

'...the glory and the memory of man will always belong to the ones who follow their great visions...'

Sir Philip Anthony Hopkins CBE (Born 31st December 1937), A Welsh Actor Of Film, Stage and Television (In Alexander, Written by Oliver Stone, Christopher Kyle and Laeta Kalogridis and Directed by Oliver Stone)

Every dream is within reach. Every vision is achievable, if only you can pay the price. So with your eyes in your head, follow the dreams of your childhood and your vision for your life. Hopefully, having paid the price in full, you would succeed, and call yourself a successful person.

The 21st Century could easily be the century for the African youth, if you would train to acquire the needed knowledge and skills to tap into the enormous opportunities it offers. If you are in school or learning a trade, or working as a professional; whatever you are doing, consider it as a route to your dreams and not only a means of earning a certificate or a monthly salary. You can readily make it as you dream. It is largely your thoughts and your will to succeed which would pave the way for you, after acquiring the needed character and skills.

There is a price for every dream. There are as many prices as there are dreams. If you dream of becoming better than Albert Einstein, you would pay a different price from the one aspiring to be better than George Oppong Weah, the next Mandela or richer than Aliko Dangote. This 'price' varies both in nature and depth.

Many of you would succeed; others may fall by the wayside. Those of you who would achieve your dreams are those who would pay the price. There are those of you, who are suited both in capacity and preparedness for the dreams so conceived. Are you willing to pay the price? If you would, can you pay the price? If your answer is yes, then you have to identify the price.

There is no doubt that, there are many challenges affecting your development towards the attainment of your dreams and aspirations. Some of the solutions to these challenges lie within your reach whilst many are beyond your grasp and control.

Note that, this book is not about dreams of the night. It is not about sentiments. It is neither about wild ambitions nor the unguided slavery to the senses and emotions. It is about planning your life, acquiring skills, vision, hard work and having a clear focus about yourself in the light of your own strength, weaknesses, the opportunities and challenges your environment may put in your way.

This book considers the social and aspirations dimensions in determining your future; a future, which should be fulfilled, dignified and prosperous.

The youth addressed in this book are those of you who, irrespective of what the society has given you or is yet to give you, have decided or would decide to give much back to the society. There are those of you who, in order to achieve your dreams, seek to understand your environment; identify how to develop your potentials and search for the sacrifices required of you. You must be patient and prepared to undergo the training needed for you to overcome challenges in your way. This will enable you acquire the required maturity which would enhance the attainment of your dreams.

The word 'dream' has been so much shouted that, it has lost much of its lustre. Many a 'motivational speakers' and 'charm doctors' have invented the word so repeatedly that its essence is largely diluted. Often, it has been glorified to be an all-in-all concept to you, without necessarily being enlightened on how to achieve it. As the case has come to be in most instances, in the light of the failure of 'dreams' to bring about the promised delights overnight, its appreciation has diminished over time and with it, is the erosion of its appeal among the youth.

Dreams should rest on reality and their attainment, on hard skills. In other words, the foundation for any successful dream is not only *the ambition* or even *the dream* itself; rather, skills and reality. That is to say, they should be grounded in common sense, where it is within reason achievable both in its essence and 'loose' time boundaries.

At the end of the day, when you say you have achieved a dream, there should be something meaningful or physical to show for it. If your dream is to be the first African to climb Mount Everest, when the dream is achieved, there should be the evidence that, you have indeed climbed the Everest.

Whatever the dream, there should be something to show for it when the sun finally sets on it. As such, even though it is important to dream, you should regularly assess these dreams on the basis of your skills, acquired knowledge and supportive environment. You should also find out the strategies and necessary support inherent in identifying what needs to be done, at which suitable time, where and how to start, and at what cost.

The traditional maxim has been: *dream big; dream for the sun and if you fail to reach the sun, you would land on the moon.* Sincerely, such views still hold and are necessary to generate enthusiasm and sustain your focus. The issue at this point is that, we are taking the 'dream big' agenda to the next and a different level.

In writing this book, I seek to embrace the position that, the youth has serious challenges to confront with more than you would imagine in your daydreaming and as such, it is important for you to live within the boundary of reason most of the time. Dreaming to become bigger than Mr Kofi Annan is not enough to make you bigger than Mr Annan. It calls for more. It takes more.

Dreams come with sacrifices. They have costs. The sacrifices as envisaged here relate to the material, emotional and social issues you would have to pay in the pursuit of your dreams. It is on this simple premise that I make an attempt to encourage you to persevere in the pursuit of a better future. A future, which would bestow on you opportunities for prosperity and better living conditions which include education, secured jobs, dignity and respect among your peers worldwide.

The future of every society is tied to the quality of its youth. The United Nations in its World Programme of Action for the Youth, agrees in the letter that, 'the imagination, ideals and energies of young people are vital for the continuing development of the societies in which they live'. As a young person, your contributions are key to the lifelong continuity of your nation.

Many of you have long lost the sparkle in your eyes as a result of unguided dreams and ambitions, which were neither rooted in reality nor common sense. Nor did you put in much effort in achieving them.

It is important to note that, life is an organized continuous journey. It is a journey requiring patience, thought, guidance, planning, sacrifices, balance and strength. It is important to create a balance between passions, sentiments and selfish ambitions on one hand, with reality on the other, if you are to succeed in life.

You Need The Right Environment

In the pursuit of a better future, many of you have had your dreams choked by a very hostile society; a society, which supports neither fresh ideas nor rewards hard work. This society does not give hope of a better tomorrow. Yes, today, many of our societies place an overly emphasis on material wealth whilst values such as dignity, hard work, honesty, compassion, respect for life, truth, and individual responsibility are neglected. Without doubt, these values, which were the bedrock of a prosperous society our founding fathers left to your fathers to improve and preserve for you, have been left to fade.

The environment haunts and breathes fear into the hearts of many of you to the extent that, you now believe that our African situation is lost. We cannot be redeemed. The dream of a better future can only be achieved in our dreams or on Western Shores. One day, I posted this simple statement on my *Facebook* wall; *'I see a Ghana where one day skyscrapers would adorn our skylines, with Toshiba and Google all having regional offices in the country'*. The responses were interesting. It was largely the belief that I was living in a different Ghana. One friend retorted; *'Boat (Boateng), what did you take for supper before bed yester night?'*

Is hope lost? That week, during lectures, I told my students that; *'I sincerely believe Ghana and many African countries would one day be like The United Kingdom or Malaysia and better'*. They 'laughed' at me. To my then students, the environment is heading towards the point of irreparability. Or we are even at that point. They believed, the environment creates darkness all around and mocks the thought of having a dream.

A dream of a better someday when you can look in the eyes of the American, the French and the Chinese and say; *'I am a Ghanaian, a Nigerian, an Egyptian, a Tanzanian or a Congolese...'* without shame and any form or dint of embarrassment.

Many of our earlier battles are lost but the War is not lost. We are winning the battle against coup d'états, we are getting our economic policies right, we are pushing back negative narratives about our continent; our economies are growing beyond the 5% mark; and the society is gradually calling for accountability from political leadership. We have a young working population. We are making progress on the many levels as well. We are definitely redeemable. We shall be there.

When you have come to the end of your drive and strength; find comfort in the inspiring line from Youssou N'Dour;

'...Africa dream again...'

As an African youth, if you have lost hope, dream again. If you have been burnt out by the pains and struggles in your countries, continue to hold on to your childhood dreams. Those of you who are untouched by your hostile environments, should dream of a loftier future. Let those of you who are fearful, never lose heart. Dream again. The failure of our fathers should rather strengthen than break you into accepting the global status quo.

You should learn from them. We should ask ourselves why they failed; how they failed and how we would succeed.

As for why we should succeed, the answer should simply lie in our quest for dignity, fulfilment, prosperity and respect among the comity of nations. Through creativity and hard work, you shall overcome and achieve this dream.

You are in different times. There is less darkness. You have better tools. You have the opportunity to be better. You are in new times and in a new age with glorious benefits. Let the former ways pass away. Do not hold on to them because they are fancy. Allow *time* to sweep them away along with the evils and misplaced resources you were enticed with to waste through unbridled materialism. You must recognise this new period and position yourselves to receive from it, as you look more within yourself with a commitment to spiritual development. There is a great and lasting future ahead.

It is important to point out that, even though the environment might be against the attainment of your dreams, you have within you what it takes to overcome and succeed. So dream again and hold on to it. Do not be weakened by doubt. Let us agree with George Benson that:

> *...It's been a long.... Long time coming .... But I know.... a change is going to come... ... yes it will... look it's here... It's been too hard living...*

The Riches Of A Nation

The riches of a nation should not be determined by its natural resources, land mass, and material wealth, but the ability of that society to create and support the right environment to help its youth (and citizens) to achieve their dreams. It must have the right institutions, leadership, value systems and attitudes. It should be a society that would make any youth who has the right skills, the right mentality and character excel. It must be a society where the youth would be free from fear of the future, unemployment, hunger, failure, poverty and lack of opportunities. The riches of a nation should be determined by the skills, knowledge, dreams and ambitions of her citizens.

Without doubt, 'as we are afraid to die' our youth need a society, rich enough to help them become whoever they want to be. Remember, an opportunity should be embraced rather than be disregarded for ephemeral pleasure associated with youthfulness.

Let us keep high hopes for Africa.

Ambition is not enough

Note that, you cannot close your eyes and hope that, when you open your eyes, your dreams would be realised. Ambition is not enough. Ambition is only a driving force. It is part of the foundation. It must be backed by real skills and character. Thus, decision-making, goal-setting and attainment of dreams should be formulated on careful thoughts. You ought to also analyse their implications in consultation with counsellors. In achieving this end, acquiring basic skills is fundamental.

Skills are the other layer of the foundation for achieving your dreams.

Whereas ambition is the fuel which powers you forward, skill is the key which steers you safely to the realisation of your dream.

Your Dreams Are Your Guide

Dreams are only dreams if not 'tempered with reality'. Your fathers had great dreams but only a few ever realised the world they so eloquently created in their minds and hearts. Why did only so few realise their dreams? You must answer this question if, indeed, you wish to go beyond the average levels many of your fathers reached.

Your dreams could be an important factor in guiding your choices in your professional and social life. On many occasions, they serve as the fire that spurs you on to overcome challenges, obstacles and failures. Sometimes, they serve as the bedrock of hope. With this hope, you overcome the challenges of your society. In times of hopelessness, your dreams console and comfort you, with the promise that, a better day would come tomorrow. In this, you would have the assurance that, you can be another Kofi Annan, Mo Ibrahim, Anta Diop, Nelson

Mandela, Kwame Nkrumah, Justice Georgina Wood, and Alhaji Malcolm Shabaz or Greater.

Greatness Has Many levels

Bear in mind that, greatness has many levels. For someone, becoming the number one tennis player in the world is his mark of greatness. Yet to another, becoming Africa's number one golfer is his mark. Still to another, becoming the best in his country is the mark. To one businessman, building a ten million Ghana Cedi business is his mark of greatness. For another, his greatness is measured by building a ten billion Naira business and with another, a hundred billion Rand business is the mark. To another person, getting an Academic Diploma Certificate is the mark for him, since he is the first in his family to achieve such a mark.

In the higher sphere of loftier ideals, my drive for proposing *big dreams* is to urge you to free your mind from small things and embrace greater goals and aspirations. The youth who created Facebook, Google, Napster and "XYZ" had no special skills in their respective discipline than you possess. So, set your horizons higher; work harder, acquire the right attitudes and be bold.

Go for it.

Believe in yourself and your dreams. Having a car, buying a house, and three square meals are not achievements. They are basic necessities. Your harsh environment has defined them to you as great achievements, thereby robbing many of you of the drive to go beyond this basic level.

It is worth creating something that would be appreciated beyond the boundaries of your society and appreciated by the world. So start small and as you do, your horizon should be to conquer the world.

Note that, the society you live in is far more sophisticated than you can understand. It is complex, cruel and unforgiving. It eats up dreams. So be careful. Cultivate patience. Take time to learn and make regular consultations with elders.

Challenges You are Likely to Face

There are large numbers of challenges in our nations. Poor education, poorly equipped skills training facilities, lack of motivation, unbridled corruption among others, hamper the ability of many of you to achieve your dreams. On the other hand, issues such as stereotypes, government policy, culture, and lack of focus could hamper your development. Let us face it, some of the problems you are facing are sometimes self-inflicted, and not largely imposed by the environment as has been widely accepted.

It is then important for you, on one hand, to redefine your dreams and aspirations and to organise your energies to define the environment to suit you. That is to say, create or influence your environment in such a way as to help you to realise your dreams and aspirations. This endeavour, reasonably, should be a collective effort.

You Need Opportunities

Part of this book is an attempt to create a platform to help you realise your dreams, analyse your environment, and finally decide how those dreams and aspirations could be achieved in the context of your peculiar environment, your skills, capacity and drive.

We are different individuals. What works for Asante may not work for Amina. So would the case of Amina be used for Ashie or Allim. Evidently, each one of you is a unique and distinct individual, requiring unique conditions towards the realisation of your aspirations.

Ultimately, I guess it is your dream to grow into a responsible adult, live in dignity and contribute to the building of your society. Such dreams are within reach; not so ambitious but modest in all intents. To these ends, you need skills, education, resources, and the necessary challenges oiled by motivation in order to succeed. Without opportunities, you would go the way those before you went: drifting into waste even though they were talented, hardworking, big dreamers and above all, self-motivated.

Other Factors could Affect Your Dreams

Dreams would be just dreams if not grounded in common sense and on a solid plan. As it is, the distance between your dreams and reality could either be a year or a lifetime's journey. Whatever your dreams are, for them to become reality is not solely in your hands. It is influenced by environmental factors, which to a large extent are influential in determining success and failure of dreams.

These factors are neither created nor controlled by you but by those who by virtue of their power and authority partly decide your rise, namely, the governments, policy makers, religious leaders, traditional authorities, mentors, role models and parents.

You would be naive to commit your destiny in the hands of those who have no real touch with the realities of the times and are not in a position to create substantial opportunities towards the attainment of youthful goals, which by design, would serve the large and loftier interests of the society. The sordid situation is that, no person or group outside your groups could do enough for you; when political promises made to commit resources to a solid youth policy is unduly delayed in its adoption, or worse, when there is no solid roadmap policy document to serve the youth. Then you can be certain that, you are not the top priority. What then shall you do in such a situation? Abandon your dreams or go forward? Certainly, you ought to go forward. You do so through innovation, improvisation and by networking and tapping into the experiences of experts and colleagues.

Two Likely Setbacks

The problem of achieving genuine drive to improve your society is in two folds. Firstly, the smaller but more active part of the society is cold-footed to usher in any era they cannot control and might have the tendency of challenging the status quo. To this end, they have adopted subtle means of keeping their interest secured. They employ innocent young people to split the youth front, while those of you who understand the environment and are well aware of its implications are too weak to act. Sometimes you are scared by the enormity of what is to be done. Largely, many young persons are coerced, threatened, scared and forced by the cold forces in the society into accepting the situation as it is, with the benign promise that, it would eventually get better. It never would get better, if you fail to act and advocate for a better society.

The second is the fact that, your front is openly divided. You are weak in your resolve and largely uncoordinated. This situation is the core of the youth underdevelopment question. You cannot be blamed for this though since you do not control the political, economic and social powers in the society. You would only be blamed if you fail to *act*. The thrust of the issue at this point is to advocate the truth of life's struggles thus; rarely does anything come on a silver platter.

As such, one has to *earn* what he seeks for by struggling against the status quo with a sustained hunger, determination and stubbornness.

Beware

Note that, when you have achieved your dreams in the course of contributing to the creation of an environment, one better in your opinion; true to history, one day, another generation would rise and would need a different form of an environment to achieve their dreams. And the struggle would begin again.

Basic Questions

In the end, it comes down to basic questions. Ask yourself, what can I do to help myself achieve my dreams? To the society, ask what it can do to help you? To the policy maker, you must ask him if his policy proposals are creating the wealth of opportunities, and right environment required for your development. And if there are 'some' policies in place, you must further ask him, can these policies enhance my aspirations? Can they help build and sustain me in the 21st century?

To the politician ask him, are you creating opportunities for me? Are your political programmes preparing me for the task of building myself and contributing to the national effort? Are you entrenching the rule of law, justice, and unity among the youth?

In answering these questions, if you are confident in your abilities and attitudes, as a young person, to the effect that you are capable of lifting the common youth interests together; if policy makers and politicians have created the right policies and institutions to serve the common interests and not special interests; if the society is serving the youth interests unbiased by creating opportunities for all based on potential and blind to ethnicity, religion and profession, then we can say that, the future of our youth is secured. Otherwise, we cannot escape the endless spiral of failures, which have become a common feature in many of our nations.

BOOK ONE

SOCIAL DIMENSIONS OF YOUR DREAMS

"Keep true to the dreams of your youth.

Johann Christoph Friedrich von Schiller
(10th November 1759 –9th May 1805)
A German Poet, Philosopher, Historian and Playwright

CHAPTER 1

THE YOUTH: WHO DO POLICIES SAY I AM?

*'Young women and men are invaluable assets that
no country can afford to waste. They bring energy,
talent and creativity to the world of work together
with new skills and the motivation that enable
companies to grow, innovate and prosper'.*

ILO

Country and Institutional Definitions

Your identity in the modern society has largely been defined
along chronological and statistical terms. The Sierra Leonean
Youth Development Policy defines the youth as those between
the ages of eighteen (18) and thirty-five (35); the United Nations
defines the youth as those within the age bracket of fifteen (15)
to twenty-four (24), whilst The Russian Governmental Decree
No. 1760-r of 18th December 2006, put the age of the youth
between fourteen (14) and thirty (30). The European Union
white paper on the youth adopted in Brussels on the 21st of
November 2006 puts the ages of the youth at between fifteen
(15) and twenty-five (25). The Ghana youth policy denotes the
ages as from fifteen (15) years to thirty-five (35) years. The
African Union Youth Charter, on the other hand, puts the ages
at between fifteen (15) and thirty-five (35).

One feature, which is obvious from the above definitions, is
the reasonably closeness of the starting and cut-off ages for
both national and international policy positions. Another
observation is the starting age of the youth, which is around

age fourteen (14) and fifteen (15). At this age, you would either be in an educational institution or a training facility acquiring knowledge and skills for life.

These definitions are, as a matter of fact, more important for social and growth planning. Largely, they do not address the peculiarities distinct to each of you. They barely give insights on your aspirations in your particular demographic area, within a particular society.

Even though definitions of the 'youth have changed continuously in response to fluctuating political, economic and socio-cultural circumstances,' at every point, they shed light on the age issue relative to your assumed collective orientation and appreciation of issues which, in principle, is necessary for any healthy policy planning and management. This is without much recourse to your individual aspirations though.

Furthermore, the age gives an idea as to your characteristics, life development, aspirations, character formation and temperament. This is based on the assumption that, chronological age has a bearing on growth and maturity in a generalised environment.

It is important to note that, this chronological age criteria used in defining you has its challenges though. The realities of your various communities, environments and life give another side, which is lofty, less dramatic, and deeper in its definition, which the chronological definition does not readily note.

Individual Differences

The environment people live in influence their growth and maturity. Two young people of the same age and same IQ in different environments are likely to exhibit characteristics peculiar to their environment. Thus, an individual in a rich environment is more likely to develop his potentials higher because of the richness of that environment and opportunities than the other in an environment with limited opportunities. Thus the definition of the youth should go beyond age to include existing policies, youth programmes, opportunities, political will, national orientation and national development agenda.

Your growth rate, maturity and opportunities would set you apart. This is well noted by authorities not excluding the Swiss psychologist, Jean Piaget. Piaget's scientific position brings into sharp focus the need to pursue an environmental definition. Thus, there seems to be a superiority of a definition based upon the opportunities, orientation and the culture over chronological age, which has largely been the yardstick of central government policies.

It is important to reconsider the culture of proposing single bracket policy for the entire categories of youth who live in different geographic locations and environments.

On your part, you should not restrict your dreams to this age limit. Nor should you allow age to dictate your development. Rather, you need to concentrate on skills development and knowledge acquisition. Point out to policy makers that, our environment is distorted in a number of ways, to the extent that, it would be a catastrophic blunder to dwell policies on the age bracket alone. Instead, there should be a careful definition of smart policies and programmes on the realities relative to each of your demographics. Thus this should be symmetrical to the relative environments within which you find yourself.

That is to say, urge that programmes should reflect our culture, and statistical underpinnings, which define the job category, aspirations, skills level, home conditions, education, and psychological orientation.

For example, a twenty (20) year old youth living in a small town called Mpasaso faces different challenges from another twenty (20) year old living in Kasulu, Kumasi, Ife metropolis or any other similar community for that matter.

It is important to urge the society to grow with time so that, it would continue to be useful in a manner in which its customs, values and way of life would continue to be useful to her youth. For this reason, join all stakeholders to act with one accord to develop, sustain and grow an environment capable of supporting your generations in your dreams and aspirations. By so doing, you would save your society and make it viable, sustainable and meaningful.

General Cultural Definition

Every society is unique on its own merits. It has different cultures, social values and opportunities such as levels of education, appreciation and availability of technology. Even in areas where these items are similar, they show remarkable distinctions in their applications.

Furthermore, societies show differences in levels of development, historical and geographical factors, demographic as well as value systems.

Factors such as wars and ethnic rules also affect how the society views and defines the youth. This in turn, informs the society on its methodology and goals to develop her youth.

A nation should define its youth in its own unique way to reflect its values, culture and aspirations. Thus, the definition should create enough space for your aspiration. What should be easily observable is that, each country defines you in terms of its peculiar situations.

Such definitions should not be dictated by chronological age, rather, by the society's preparedness and appreciations, political and labour systems, and to a large extent, its history and vision for the future.

Furthermore, the economic capacity of the society and how much of its resources are made available to your development are also critical. One very important issue, though recurrent, concerns the highest political authority in the society. It is necessary to ascertain their commitment to a youth policy, their ideological leaning and how much political risk they are prepared to take towards a realistic and effective youth course. Thus, if a society has a view of creating professionals in information technology it would set herself up to develop the youth along these lines in order to serve that need without recourse to endless talk shops and lack of focus.

Your traditional environment is fraught with many considerations. It is important to note that, most cultural definitions tend to focus more on mental appreciation, skills acquisition, physiological maturation and knowledge rather than on the chronological age. It is more of a generational classification. Most traditional environments dictate that, this stage is the period of learning the ways of the society, dealing with elders, co-habitation, skills acquisition, survival skills, contributions to the society and any other skills needed for you to grow into a good citizen. The generational cap was prominent when traditional form of education was the sole route for preparing you for future service to the society. You were considered in terms of generations and not by age bracket.

In the modern dispensation, formal education has taken prominence over traditional education in your grooming. This situation could partly be as a result of the inability of traditional education to embrace all manner of youth under one umbrella within the society.

Furthermore, the inflexibility of traditional education to adapt and break cultural barriers was a serious challenge under statehood with a uniform educational model.

The chronological age has become more prominent in the classification of the youth than using a system based upon skills acquisition, orientation, value system and generational cap. This is largely by the fact that, there is no uniform scientific system in place, under the traditional education system, to generally measure the skills level and standardise value systems across societies to come out with a common yardstick acceptable by all. Furthermore, the traditional education system is generally difficult to accept under a central government, which has subordinated all traditional educational structures.

In the process, central government has taken the burden of youth development out of the hands of traditional leaders with the aim of creating a common youth for the nation; a youth who sees himself as a member of a nation first, rather than an Asante, a Bissa, a Shona, a Yoruba or a Hutu or Tutsi.

This statement could be better put when one considers the fact that, the nation is the sum of smaller societies and that to leave the grooming of the youth to these smaller states would present a form of confusion, which would serve the interest of the individual communities at the expense of the Nation. This could lead to imbalances in levels of development. This is not to ignore the fact that, even with a common national youth policy, there are disparities in development as a result of historical, capacity, geographical and cultural concerns.

It is important to mention that, the pre-statehood societal system was not flawed in its inability to produce a youth capable of surviving beyond his society. Rather, training had been dictated to by the needs and aspirations of each society.

Along these needs had come with different types of training philosophies and character measurements. The challenge, in the light of a national society, was the lack of uniformity in those measurements.

Character versus Paper Certificate

The traditional education prepared you beyond skills to acquire character and values to enable you to contribute fully to meet the needs and challenges the society faced whereas the current educational and skills training environment emphasise more on academic knowledge. The existing educational environment would not allow for adequate character preparation for life nor test the same in the real world, largely, as a result of syllabi restrictions and school term limitations.

The society place emphasis on the paper certificate than ask if you are prepared on all dimensions of life.

The measurement and assessment of character at its terminal points through academic examinations is not enough. You could always write excellently to pass examinations without necessarily adhering to true values. The observations of teachers and counsellors at the end of the educational period to parents as being done on a term basis give insight to parents on your conduct and would make only a limited impact even if acted upon.

In the traditional society, the nuggets of wise counsels given by the 'fire side', on the farm path and at dawn were followed up by close observation by parents, family and the community to ensure that, they had become part of your life.

Is the society to be blamed?

These observations made above are not as a result of poor or lack of policy; rather, the current society is asymmetrical towards character formation. Thus you take more bad habits and attitudes from a corrupted society than you do from books in the educational system to form a proper character. The society does not present a clear picture of you to allow for concrete programmes to address your aspirations and challenges. Thus, without question, the present system does not prepare you for these challenges within the stipulated age as defined in policy papers.

It is important to note that, each nation has different visions for the youth. Even though there are lines of similarity among such definitions, the state sees (defines, assigns roles, inculcates values, grooms) you in a way reflective of its needs and dreams. Since aspirations and goals of societies vary from one society to the other, it is understandable that you are seen in an environmental as well as chronological age scope rather than in a chronological-age scope alone.

It is significant to recognise that, the age brackets denoted by national youth policies are just ages, with their lofty underpinnings implied in an ideal environment, which does not exist in reality. The real issue is the recognition of the fact that, skills development and value systems should be the guiding light of every society.

There are exceptions, which require brief comments though, with respect to the age issue. By virtue of individual differences, one may well be below the age of thirty (30) but would be so matured that he might not need any support targeted for the young. So it is on the other hand that, someone well above the age of thirty-five (35) may need youth support programmes as a seventeen-year old youth would require. These exceptional issues abound in reality.

Know Your Limitations

It is important for you to learn your limitations, level of maturity and the requirements of your dream. Policy makers and society on the other hand, have a moral duty to have a workable youth policy; bearing in mind that, their sacred duty is not to those of you who by virtue of birth, circumstances or chance are well positioned to survive on your own, but to the vulnerable and the weak; those lacking in skills, knowledge and direction.

You need to make sure that, policy makers hear this message.

A Requirement of a Youth Policy

It is important for you to note that, a national youth policy that does not take the peculiar needs of various societies and their cultural sensitivities into account would not suffice. Various ethnic groups have different cultures, level of development and values that define their particular environment. In Ghana, Northern Region is quite unique from the Western Region in many ways including social, economic, religious and cultural issues. Even within the Western Region, the Aowins are different in many aspects from the Jomoros. So are the Dagombas of the Northern Region different from the Gonjas. Their culture, value systems and geography among others, are different.

The rich fertile lands of the Western Region would offer the youth ready access to a prosperous career in cocoa farming and related secondary and tertiary industries. Additionally, industrial citing as a result of the rich minerals of the Western Region, educational institutions and other economic activities clearly separate the youth in this region by way of opportunities and attitudes from those of the Northern Region.

On the other hand, the North cannot be said to have such fertile lands for cocoa or lumber and thriving mining economic activities as the Western Region. Even the land ownership systems are quite different. Additionally, issues such as social and ethnic dynamics within such communities distinguish this environment from others. This notwithstanding, soil type of the North makes it suitable for yam, shea-butter and guinea fowl farming. Thus, secondary and tertiary industries in shea-butter and yam are more suitable there than they would thrive in the Western Region.

These distinctions could be identified in various communities. The actors within these communities define the environment and thus affect you in your orientations and eventual development. For this reason, you should urge that, policy should be deliberate, specific and programmes to implement the policies painstakingly designed to ensure that, these specific environmental factors are rather the baseline for policies and not age alone.

CHAPTER 2

YOUR ROLES AND RESPONSIBILITIES IN NATION BUILDING

'Young people are our future but also our present. The opportunities that are being created for young people today lay the foundations for what economies they will be able to achieve tomorrow'.

ILO

Your Traditional Roles In the Society

There is no doubt that young people in all countries are both a major human resource for development and key agents for social change, economic development and technological innovation. They are a bridge between the old, the present and the future, as well as carrying the torch of the society defined by their cultures and values.

Traditionally, the youth undertook many roles in the home and society. You were one of the most important members of the society for social and economic development. In the traditional society, you were needed for communal work, farm hands, fighting force or for any chores, which the elderly deemed fit and necessary for the good of the society. You were also considered as students and units for sustainability. The youth were indeed the life of the society. For these reasons, among others, greater care and pain were taken in your upbringing.

Their needs were taken as the responsibility of the society. For practical reasons, instead of looking at individual cases alone, the society created an environment that served the larger group interests whilst paying close attention to peculiar individual youth needs.

In furtherance of the aim of building you in a wholesome manner, games, value systems, traditions and taboos were created to grow, polish and preserve a suitable environment. Suffice to say, it is indeed important to note that, individualism was key in attaining livelihood skills such as hunting, blacksmithing and sports such as wrestling but the resultant benefit from these skills were to serve the society and help you to contribute to its wellbeing.

Your, virgin minds were moulded to provide societal needs. In other words, among others, you provided what the older society could not do or secure in order to balance the society in its social, military, economic and political needs.

It is important for you to be aware of your role, understand your environment, the limitations of the same and to a large extent, ascertain how you could influence it. Additionally, it is important for you to understand the environment for the purpose of charting a realistic course for your dreams. As such, it is not enough for the youth to have dreams. Your roles in transforming your environment to create the necessary opportunities for yourself should be equally important. It is insightful to observe that, your roles have never been static. It has evolved with time, technology, aspirations (of the youth), and ideals of the society.

Some of your Traditional roles included:

Bearers of Values

In our traditional society, your roles were complementary to the roles of other members of the society. Largely you also served as the bearers of the values, identity and the dreams of the society. You are mouldable, and as such a vital component of the society.

Your leaders then were wise and proved they had the society's stability and future at heart. You were bred in values which served the society and shed good light on the genuine actions of the elders. Even in cases where coercion was applied, as sometimes in marriages, it was seen to be for the greater and common good of families and society.

If the gong-gong was beaten for clearing of the stream-path, those who failed to respond were punished severely. The severity of the punishment was subordinated to the 'crime' of refusing to take part in a meaningful duty to the society. Greed, gluttony, selfishness, dishonesty and related bad attitudes were all abhorred by the society because they contribute to the erosion of trust and the foundation of the society.

Manpower Roles

Your roles, which were sometimes supplementary, in providing manpower base for the society is well known. You served as the supplementary base providing the physical strength needed to provide the needs of the society. These needs included food production, building of community centres, places of convenience, schools, clearing of farm route, maintenance of bridges, cleaning of water sources, sweeping of refuse sites, clearing of gutters, and any manner of humane physical labours the society needed and required. These were largely undertaken under guidance of elders. Suffice to say, you performed these roles as were necessary for the balance of labour within the society.

You Were Part of the Fighting Force

Critically, one of your roles was in providing the central fighting force in times of tribal and societal feuds. Believing in the order and sanctity of the society in an era where wars and raids were prevalent, the male youth was most valued to serve as the support force and a wall of defense for the society. First defending the societal lands, citizens, and properties, and secondly attacking enemies and raiding rounds. In other words, you served as part of the shield for protecting the entire community.

You formed part of the Asafo Company

You also formed the basic unit of Asafo companies. Asafo companies had diverse roles in our societies. You were motivated and resourced to serve the community in times of crisis and need. You portrayed the spirit of selflessness, communality and sacrifice. When someone lost his way in the forest, they would rise to search and bring him home. If a wild animal strayed from the forest to their homes, they would rise to either kill or drive it back.

If a tribe captured a citizen, the Asafo Company would rise up in arms to bring her back. In wartime, the Asafo Company was an integral part of the fighting force. Thus, you were truly such an important member of the society. It is said that, it was worth 'seeing the pride in the eyes of the youth as they carried a found person from the forest amidst singing and Drumming'.

The opposite was equally sad when they failed in their bid to rescue a member of the society on whose behalf they rose to defend. Their sad faces summed up their pain that, they have failed their society. When a stream swept away a foot-bridge, the energy and enthusiasm with which the Asafo Company responded to the call of the gong-gong was most envious. It was a beautiful sight to behold, knowing that, you belonged to a society which would respond to a call on your behalf in times of need. It is worth noting that, through the Asafo Company the youth learnt values such as communality, selflessness, heroism, courage, trust, and the art of survival.

Roles as Good Wives and Educators

The muscular work of the roles of the youth tends to overshadows the role of the female youth in the society. You were needed for a number of critical chores. You were required to be good wives, giving assistance to your husbands, keeping the home, performing less muscular work on the farm, child-bearing and teaching the values of the society to your children.

Suffice to say, the woman was seen as a partner and a helper to the man. In this regard, mothers sought to train their daughters how best to offer their roles. Furthermore, you were educated in the values the society required of you as would-be mothers, to be the informer and enforcer of knowledge and values to your children. These values, of course, included universal values such as hard work, dignity, generosity, humility, love and unity.

Child Bearing

Traditionally, the place of the woman had been at the home and soft jobs. Indeed, reproduction, a vital requirement in the society, was a key role of the woman to continue the lineage of families. It is not difficult for the woman to incur the displeasure and wrath of the family if she was perceived as barren.

It is important to note that, the modern society makes little distinction between the male and female youth in the manner the traditional society did.

Partly, it is as a result of the general roles expected of you, which is less muscular, and more of soft skills. The female has also changed in mentality and has thus conditioned herself to take on traditionally male categorised roles such as owning farms, houses, and leadership roles. In Ghana, the name Yaa Asantewaa has come to symbolise this new woman, the liberated woman.

Preservation of Family Trade

You were not always for physical endeavours. The training of your minds was also important to the society. Many of you were trained in family trades to preserve professional skills and to add to it through innovation. The society expected each family to pass on its trade to you and consequently, you on the other hand, to serve the society with the skills acquired. So the hunter trained his son to be a better hunter, the blacksmith did the same and the chief taught the children of his court the art of diplomacy, mercy, justice and leadership.

You were at the Centre of Knowledge Transfer

It is important to state that, knowledge transfer and skills training were bedrocks for the preservation and expansion of knowledge. You were at the centre of these transfers. This made you all the more important in your societies. In pursuit of these endeavours, the necessary opportunities were provided for you in acquiring necessary skills and improving responsibilities required of you.

Strength and Agility

Beyond chores on farming and as helping hands, wrestling matches were organised to ensure strength and agility. More importantly, these wrestling sports were to instil the virtues of competition and to challenge you to aspire to be the best. The belief was that, competition would bring the best in you. It is told that, these sporting spectacles were also grounds for bride-matching and winners usually won the hearts of the most beautiful women in the community.

Wisdom and Maturity

Storytelling and proverbs were all encouraged to ensure that, qualities such as wisdom, knowledge, and social values which sports and associations could not imbue in you were learnt. Furthermore, it was used to tell the history of the society and its folklore to you and the future generation.

One critical role of these other activities was to provide an opportunity for those of you who could not compete in the games nor join an Asafo Company but were good storytellers and other soft skills to identify their trade and develop it. Indeed, your total development for you to perform your obligations satisfactorily to the society was taken seriously.

Your Roles In the Modern Society:

In the modern society, your roles could be categorised under social, civic, professional and cultural. These fall under the dimensions of sustainability, growth and protection of the society. The current environment, aided by time, technology, inventions, innovation, the creation of nationhood and changes in the needs of societies and the nation, have imposed a set of new obligations on you. There are no tribal wars to be fought. The role of physical strength as was required for war and aggression have all been relegated to the fringes. No healthy society sees war and aggression as a basic requirement for its survival. Skills acquisition and employment of the same are now universal. You are no longer restricted to your community in the pursuit of either the acquisition of skills or employment. New ways of learning are now vested in formal education and open apprenticeship. It is even wider and more accessible to acquire skills for the job market.

Government policies have also contributed to your new roles through national vision and youth policies. It is worth stating that, these policies and programmes should not increase the challenges you are already facing though. They should rather increase your opportunities. This is because on your shoulders lay the manpower base of the nation and the medium and long term intellectual base for development. In the light of this, it is important to 'encourage (your) participation in social, economic and political activities of the society'.

The gap between the conditions of these modern times and the inadequacies of policies, programmes and institutions of the society are of much worry and indeed create room for dropouts and delinquents.

The roles of the youth in the life of the society are now more diversified than they were three decades ago. These roles are now more intellectual than manual.

Despite these changes, your roles have only increased and gained more prominence. A large regular military force and police services are required. This means that the nation needs soldiers, policemen who should not only be young but intellectually capable enough to deliver the roles required of them.

Our educational needs are greater and diversified. The size and diversity of the economy and government require all manner of personnel. Your roles are even more complicated under the concepts of globalisation of knowledge, capital, resources and interests.

These are challenging times for parents, traditional authorities and policy makers. The basic question to ask in the light of these fundamental changes is that, are there enough guidance, resources, willingness and the goodwill on the part of those holding the power nerve, from the nuclear and extended family, community and nation, to commit themselves to the enormous task of training the 21st century African youth?

Itemizing Your Modern Roles as thus (*These roles could, in a way, extend to all citizens*).

Placing Your Acquired Knowledge at the Disposal of the Society

Your modern roles are not dependent on the historical, cultural and the requirements of your immediate environment alone. Irrespective of your societal past, economic, political and cultural environment, it is incumbent upon you not only to contribute to building yourself but to help in building the society in many ways. These may include information dissemination, education in certain key areas such as HIV/AIDS, sanitation, among others.

These cannot be said to be daunting tasks, partly because at your young age, by accident of time, you may have acquired skills and knowledge your parents did not acquire when they were at your present age. With orientation, you would recognise that you are capable of performing the roles society and time have obligated you with.

By dedicating yourself to the service of the community, you would be fulfilling an age-old value of your society; a core responsibility to foster goodwill known as sacrifice, which had been one of the bedrocks of our society. That is to say, you owe it to your society to sacrifice towards building it. It is a noble sacrifice for you to commit your energies, time, knowledge and other resources to help the community in whichever way you can.

It is imperative to add that, the acquisition of knowledge is not enough for you to be useful to the society if you are not willing to use that knowledge for the welfare of the nation. Therefore, for the good of the society, it is important for you to recognise that, you need to go beyond to the higher level, where you give back to the society, irrespective of what the society has given to you so far. In this regard, it is expected that, you should give back to the society as much as it gives you. It is a reciprocal rule.

This would not be an easy decision for you to make in an environment where greed and selfishness are in the open. Yet, irrespective of these flaws and against the backdrop that, this society might have given so many of you very little, it is important to urge you to have a big heart and to be heroes as you save many with your skills and resources and new found knowledge.

It is important to also note that, in helping the society, you should consider areas outside your professions. It is not a compulsory call. Rather, it is an appeal to you to help the disadvantaged in the society. It must not necessarily be money in this instance, but the sharing of knowledge and the society would do better with your knowledge in key areas of need. For instance, folks in the village would do with education on HIV /AIDS, Guinea worm eradication, scientific farming practices, hygiene and fighting malaria.

You offer the most virgin mind for creating, sustaining and driving projects of national priority. This position, of course, leaves out the role of policy. And as it is the situation with many governments, youth policy has been lingering on third rate issues of governments' agenda.

Our founding fathers: Dr Kwame Nkrumah, Nelson Mandela, Abdul Nasser, J.B. Danquah, Patrice Lumumba, Tafawa Belewa, took a lot of risks and sacrifices at the peril of their lives, livelihood, freedom and liberties to secure their nations. In these shining examples lies a responsibility for you to emulate. Although some of them did not live to witness the fruit of their sacrifices, our political independence, freedoms and our modest development attest to the selfless spirit of those noble souls among them, who today inspire millions.

In this era of extreme greed, selfishness, mediocrity and materialism, it is difficult to urge you to be selfless and sacrifice for the common good. Yet the call has to be made though. Despite this fact, it is important for you to remember that, one should always be guided by the actions of heroes, patriots and 'Big` minds rather than the actions and deeds of mean and little men; men who live for themselves and immediate families alone; men who do not see the beauty of sacrifice, honour, dignity, generosity and fighting for the weak in the society; men to whom money, wealth and power have become a form of ruthless god.

These little men may seem happy and fulfilled but they are empty, with neither honour nor lasting legacy. They are only heroes in the fragile society they have created; a society where neither dignity nor honesty is cherished. And soon when their fragile society is exposed, they would be seen and remembered as little men. Yes, time will forever remember them little. Do not learn from them nor envy them. Look within yourself for strength and inspiration. So, 'in the spirit of tomorrow' and a prosperous future, look beyond these little men of today and offer yourselves to the society. This should be the beauty and burden of *patriotism* as you strive to leave the old nation and her grave flaws behind in pursuit of a society you would be proud of.

Today, believing in the country is a burden even dreamers cannot readily bear. There is not much to inspire patriotism. There is much to lure you into hating your very society; the creation of our hands. Today, you are left with little to believe in.

Some generations created the present society. I can only urge you to believe in the future of the nation; a future nation where you would not be scared of malaria or homelessness or poverty or unemployment. A future we can definitely achieve. And so, from where you 'stand today' resolve to absolve yourself from deeds and actions such as corruption, laziness and wickedness, which have created and nourished this society we all detest.

So fight. Fight with weapons the might of man cannot destroy. Let us fight with weapons created by not the might of man but by the hand of a divine God. Fight with truth, honesty, grace, humility, knowledge, dedication, hard work and have faith in your creator that, soon, there would be a Ghana, a Nigeria or an Egypt or a Guinea Bissau you would be proud of to call your own.

I urge you to chart a course for yourselves which would create a society you can be proud of. And to the old order, the call here is for a rebirth. The rebirth of the mind, future actions and remembering the founding days, as we anticipate that, we would triumph over mediocrity, cowardice, poor leadership and purposelessness.

Indeed, sacrificing for one's society is more rewarding than the endless pursuit of individual interests and material wealth. It is rewarding to give back to the society, even if the society gave little or nothing to you.

This society defines you as much as it creates the rich environment you would need to achieve your aspirations. You need an environment, which would give you the energy and inspire you to dream big and aim high while offering you the opportunities to achieve those dreams.

At your youthful stage, it would be quite ambitious to say you could do much to help so many. The essence of the query here is the need to acknowledge that, whatever you have, it is a national duty to give something back to those who need it. For instance, in recent years, youth groups have taken to social work by providing vacation classes, health education, rebuilding of community centres and other projects in rural and deprived areas.

Everyone has something to offer. Thus, on individual level something could be done no matter how insignificant it may seem to you at the time.

The Society Expects You to Get Education (Formal or Informal)

Knowledge is key to the development of every nation. It is your duty to acquire knowledge for your personal development and secondly, for the development of the nation. Personal knowledge is important in this era where the world has moved into areas which requires that, for you to survive you would have to acquire greater and different forms of knowledge other than those acquired by your parents or earlier generations.

In the light of this and for the good of the nation, it behoves you to recognise that, knowledge acquisition in new sciences such as Information Technology, Microbiology, Entrepreneurship and Leadership among others is a responsibility. The nation needs your drive, energy, ambition, fresh mind, innocence and all your potentials in building that genuine knowledge bank necessary to build the *New Africa* which, Dr Kwame Nkrumah, Julius Nyerere, Patrice Lumumba, Abubakar Tafawa Belewa, Abdul Nasser, Jomo Kenyatta and our founding fathers saw and sought to create.

The acknowledgement of the need to acquire knowledge (skills/education) should not be seen as a means to acquiring a certificate or status, but a means of acquiring the necessary skills base to achieving your dreams and being an active and productive member of the society.

This should be the basis for education. You have a responsibility to acquire and enhance education when the opportunity is made available. For you to attain your dreams, you need the requisite brain power, confidence and articulation.

It is worth noting that, sometimes the opportunities you would require to develop might not always be made available in a manner you so wished. Sometimes you would have to ask for them. At other times you would have to search for them. Occasionally, you have to bang on doors and fight for them with non violent and non extreme means, because there is so much at stake for you and the society.

Challenging times, locked doors and hopelessness should not be dead ends. These hurdles should not lead to the end of your dreams nor the journey to acquire the necessary knowledge base. Be bold and stand on a platform of optimism. Listen to the voice within you crying for your dreams to materialise. This voice would drive and energise you. Do not let the dream and ambition be silenced by excuses, fear, and weaknesses. Let perseverance calm you through counsel and move forward in courage, hope and hard work, discipline and commitment.

So cry for Education. Cry for freedom. Yearn for liberty. Cry for freedom from fear, laziness, and depravity. Cry for salvation, and let truth, honesty, hard work, humility and favour set your soul and body free to pursue your dreams and break free from poverty, desperation and anger which seem to encircle you.

Lack of opportunity should not be the end; for there is always an opportunity for you to develop yourself. As someone said, "There is nothing like a dead end." Just look harder than you are looking. Ask harder with the right questions and knock on the right doors. There are cases where young people from slumps have made it to the top. There are cases where young men from conflict areas, orphans and those with disabilities and tense disadvantages have made it to their dreams.

The journey towards the acquisition of knowledge should neither be determined by the abundance of opportunities nor the lack of it. You have the sole responsibility to acquire the knowledge base necessary for attaining your dreams and these dreams should not be selfish but communal. What is also essential is the orientation to seek knowledge.

Recognition of Your Place and Role in the Society

Additionally, it is your responsibility to recognize your role in society and thus build or employ yourself to honour such roles. It is under this condition that you would enhance (your) participation in the society. For even though the art of building a society is now skill-based, without the recognition to play your expected roles, whatever skills so acquired would be useless to the society as long as it is not geared towards building it in a meaningful way.

Retraining to Acquire the Needed Skills

There is another view which deals with the acquisition of skills but from a different angle. Sometimes you may have the adequate skills but it is not in the areas you wish to pursue in life. In a situation where you do not have the skills needed for the desired area but wish to contribute your quota, it is important for you to re-train for the sole purpose of acquiring the skills needed. For instance, you might have been trained as an accountant but it has become necessary for you to work as an auditor. In such an instance, it is necessary to train as an auditor for you to be able to be the auditor you wish to be. Time is not a factor here. What is important is the fact that, you are acquiring the skills to achieve a dream, a purpose and a goal. There should be neither regret nor embarrassment in retraining. It is a common practice in career shifts. It is a normal practice of life. The society needs you to be an active player in her affairs.

Be An Active Participant in the Affairs of the Community

By way of being an active player in the society, there are three obligations in mind here. These are:

1. Help in building a society that is able to make a smooth progressive movement towards new levels without distorting its existing structures;

2. Support in preserving the society. By this, you are required to uphold the values of your society; and lastly,

3. Contribute to societal correctness. By this, you are required to use your acquired new and frontier knowledge to break age-old inhibitive cultures and attitudes which are holding the society back.

In fulfilling your obligations to the society, do not wait for an ideal condition. There could never be an ideal situation. There are always challenges to overcome and responsibilities to honour. The nation needs your energies, diversities, enthusiasm and knowledge to preserve and bring in new knowledge to move it forward.

The challenges you may face in acquiring the requisite education and skills needed in honouring your obligation to the nation should not be counted as an unnecessary bother. Rather, they should, to a large extent, help you to break barriers as well as broaden your outlook and horizon. The right Education is a personal gain for you and collectively to the nation and without it, you cannot be an active participant in the affairs of the society even if you so wish to.

You need to identify that, the acquisition of knowledge for national development should not only be in the arts and sciences and or related disciplines. Rather it should critically also be in your culture and ideals. As a young Asante, Hausa, Kikuyu, Zulu or Luba, you should note that it is your duty to acquire knowledge about your traditions and ideals. This is not only for the purpose of identification and learning but also for the purpose of transformation and personal development.

By personal development, it means acquiring the age-old wisdom in our values such as honesty, integrity, hard work, respect, humility, generosity, and using them as a foundation of your character and your life. Above all, you are expected to embody the collective ideals of the nation.

As you acquire skills and knowledge to pursue your dreams, it is important also to underline that, knowledge acquisition should be universal in nature, not only for personal pursuits but also for the sustainability and growth of value systems of the nation. Thus, you should read broadly on other subject areas which might not have direct bearing on your area of specialty.

Although dreams may be diverse, as a society, if we are bound by common beliefs in our continent's intellectual and security aspirations; these diversities should only tend to strengthen the continent and our prosperity.

For as diverse as our national needs are, this dynamic nature of our aspiration would thus fuel us to build a continent of ideas, resources and opportunities and make it better for all.

In such an atmosphere, we would only entrench the belief that our society is a nation of ideas and whoever you are, whatever your ideas, provided they are not for your welfare alone, you would be encouraged to develop them. This is the dream. Participate in this dream.

Taking Up Employment or Creating a Job

You are the workforce, which operates various fields of endeavour by virtue of your energy and enthusiasm. You constitute the force for both physically and mentally oriented base jobs to create the output base necessary to move the nation forward. In this light, the acquisition of skills, knowledge, ambition, drive and capital resources are necessary but not enough.

It is important for you to employ these capacities into creating wealth and value for the society. In ensuring the constant flow of manpower resources, it is important for you to be regularly aware that, you are the human link between the very young and the retiring age groups of the society. Note that, your output is the source of wealth sustaining the society. In your field of work, one and only one mission is necessary: to employ your resources to those in need and for your personal benefit which would eventually build and sustain the society. Thus, it is important for you to work hard in entrepreneurial ventures and employment endeavours.

Payment of Taxes

Thieves, armed robbers are easily made out because of the nature of their jobs. Non payment of taxes is a form of robbery. Taxes are one of the major sources of revenue for the government. With these revenues, the society builds institutions and infrastructure to support development. Taxes are easily avoided and evaded in an environment where the rules are loose and monitoring is weak. You do not need iron-clad laws to force you to pay your taxes as a responsible member of the community.

Furthermore, you have an advocacy duty in the payment of taxes and other legal revenues. Thus you are supposed to not only pay taxes but encourage friends, colleagues and other members of the society to honour this obligation.

Thirdly, you are required to expose persons or businesses which are either avoiding or under declaring taxes. Remember that, the schools, training centres and the programmes required to help you to achieve your dreams are funded by taxes.

Avoidance of and Fight Against Corruption

Undoubtedly, corruption is an alarmingly growing disease in the society. Whether you call it lobbying, bribery or theft, it still carries with it the heavy toll of blinding public officials and affecting the national psyche. It is important for you to set the pace in honesty, and truthfulness by avoiding the lure of cheap money that tends to rob the nation. Furthermore, as usual, you are obliged to report and expose practices of corruption inherent in public services and industry. You are also expected to help agencies in fighting corruption in any way you are capable. This is your act of patriotism to the motherland.

Respecting the Values of Your Society

Another key area affecting our foundation as a society is the disrespect for some of our key values as a society which all major religions of the world support unlimitedly. These include respect for the elderly, respect for life, respect for living things, humility, generosity, hard work, love of peace, avoidance of war, communal living and other rich values within our cultural systems.

Furthermore, respect for nature, as in protecting river bodies, the forest cover and the environment. You should not only be a champion of these values you must practice and make them part of your character and being.

Following Proper Marriage Rites

The need for you, male or female, to honour the family and society by going through the proper rites before child birth is a responsibility to the society. Proper marriage rites are a duty. It is a requirement of our culture. This constitutes a critical area of our value systems and you are advised to oblige. Marriage is an institution which brings families and societies together. It is one of the basic building blocks of our society.

Cultural Agents

The values, identity and the larger culture of the society ought to be carried from one generation to the other. You have a unique role in this arena. You have a duty to learn the culture, values and the traditions of your people and pass them on to the next generation. This function could only be performed when you learn the culture and value systems of your society. Like any other member of the society, you personify these values, and by living through them, you portray the best of your society and promote them to the world. These could be a tool for fighting abrasive and empty external cultural influences which having 'conquered' many of you, have made you subservient to those cultures and their value systems, thereby adulterating and decimating our value systems and to some extent, the foundations of our society. Through widespread travel, the internet, online chat rooms and social network sites, you could showcase the best of your society to the world.

Fields of endeavour and contacts could also be an avenue for you to announce your values. For example, through your academic writings, you could use your expertise and research endeavours to promote your values. The business class, sportsmen and tourists in your international contacts could promote the values of our society.

In effect, you are not only expected to perform your traditional role of learning and acquiring the basics of society. You are further required, as a national duty, to promote these values to the outside society. *Cultural marketing* is as much a worthy national duty as your involvement in social work in your respective communities. There is so much in our culture to be proud of and so much as to market them to the world.

Our marriage ceremonies, puberty rites and their essence, festivals, naming ceremonies are unique and hold much meaning and wisdom for the world. You are our greatest Ambassador.

Reproductive Roles

The continuity of family lineage and the growth of the society is one of your cardinal functions. One of your roles is reproduction. From the beginning of societies, the youth has been the source of reproduction and continuation of the lineage in the society. The society looks up to you to continue your family lineage. Indeed, there is not much argument against your role in reproduction. In order to fulfil this duty, you are expected to keep yourself healthy and prepared psychologically and economically.

Time has really changed two dimensions of this role though. Hitherto, the need was to produce large numbers of children; mass production. The higher the number of your children, the more respected you were. This norm has changed. Today, even in our traditional societies, a child or two would suffice. Part of the society no longer sees it as a curse or a taboo to practice birth control.

The second change is the shift from male children. The norm was that, male children were regarded as more useful than females in many communities. Perhaps it was as a result of war and aggression and farm labour in those days. Today, we view both sexes as useful members of the society. Duties have inter-mixed and specialized roles have emerged for both sexes.

You are expected to be Good Parents

The birth of children is not enough for the society. There are high expectations and responsibilities that, children are brought up in the ways of our fathers: respect for the elderly, honesty and among others, respect for human life. This means that, as a would-be father or mother you ought to be able to train the child properly.

This requires maturity on your part to be able to perform these functions. As such, you are expected not to be only physically matured to get married but more importantly, to be emotionally and spiritually matured as well. Every parent has the moral obligation to train their children to be better citizens.

By the nature of the set up of our societies, a child is the 'property' of the society. So, to a large extent, the upbringing of children becomes the burden of the society. This notwithstanding, the mother (or father) is expected to be the first guardian of the child.

Partly, it is for this reason that the society seeks to ensure that, you reach a certain maturity level before taking on fatherly and motherly roles. This has less to do with age. There is much more expected of a mother or a father than the sensual pleasures which tend to drive many people.

The easiest part of motherhood and fatherhood is the sexual interactions and impulses, affections and carnal romances. Psychological pulses which characterize parenthood are normally lost to you. There are pressures, guardianship concerns, economic and emotional issues related to parenting. For these reasons, society seeks to build you to be matured for these roles before marriage. These are normally done through coaching, counselling, strict disciplinary codes and dawn-talks.

The society expects you not only to give birth to children, but also to ensure that those children are contributors of knowledge, development, and wealth creation and not as thugs, criminals, and weaklings.

Technology, which has made it more than ever possible for many of you who would have otherwise been barren, has also widened the breadth and deepened the task of parenthood.

The magic of technology empowers and imperils. It offers you with unrivalled source of cheap information for many spheres of your life: education, religion, sports and growth. It also allows you to communicate with your peers around the world and to share information and learn freely. Sometimes you can learn bad stuff.

In a split moment of blindness, any parent could lose his child. This makes parenting for your generation very daunting, much more so for the extended family and society.

The speed of technology has increased the rate of spread of bad attitudes and degradation of morality. Bad habits are spread rapidly unchecked or evenly more fairly to parents, impossible for them to check. In the era of the larger internet and social media, it is difficult to ascertain how parents could check you from overly negative influences from the net. This makes the art of parenting to the current youth the more difficult and expensive. As such, it is not an exaggeration to strongly urge that you ought to be fully matured and be prepared to train a child before embarking on any marriage adventure.

Leadership Roles

You are the most naturally endowed in every society. You are energetic, big dreamers, virgin minds and fearless. Your place in the nation has never been in doubt. This makes you a key part of the society.

We shall address one particular type of youth. These are a few selfless, magnanimous, broad minded and , above all, charismatic and likeable among them. These obviously in one way or the other, turn out as leaders in political, religious, business, traditional and priesthood spheres. This class of youth who by wish or design happens to be at the service of their peers, have a role to bear the leadership torch and burdens of the nation. The message is that, as much as anything else, you have a duty to the nation to belong to one of the faces of the nation, and go beyond that to learn, grow and be ready at the appropriate time to be one of the torch bearers of that profession to help build a better society.

A time would eventually come when the old would fade or retire. At that moment, you would be called upon to be the next leaders. When the time comes, you might not be a young man anymore but the fact still remains that, what you would have learnt 'fifteen' years ago would be a good foundation for your new role as a leader of men.

Leadership is one of your functions and there is no better time to learn and improve your leadership skills than at your youthful age. Reading literature on leadership is not the key. It is primarily acquired through taking leadership roles in school, work places, communities and churches and other avenues of endeavour.

An important note: on the outside, it may seem that the political youth is most blessed and most fortunate, perhaps because of the image you carry, as you rub hands with the powers of the land. It is not so in reality. You are most vulnerable, lonely, insecure and above all roughly treated. Yet you must bear the rough and tumble of real time leadership training, taking all the risks, making a countless number of enemies you neither know nor could handle.

Despite these uncertainties, it is important to note that, some of you should take these risks and avail yourselves to go through the uncertainties of leadership in your respective life endeavours. With proper training, adherence to leadership values, independence of thought and uniqueness, you could endear yourself to the public and constituents. Already in Rwanda, Togo, Kenya, Ghana and many African countries, we have many young persons in leadership positions in political, business, the clergy and other endeavours.

Since their rise is not in discussion, we would not consider them. Suffice to say, if you take the extra mile to trace their achievements, you would find out that, sheer ambition was not the only factor in their rise. Above all, hard work, acquisition of knowledge, humility, and patience played key roles in their rise.

In effect, you need to prepare yourself for leadership positions in the society: politics, commerce, trade, entertainment, and clergy. As the workforce age, it is important for some of you to fill their space. That is to say, you ought to go beyond the knowledge circle and acquire the leadership skills, temperament, attitudes and the necessary base to provide the needed strength and capacity for leadership roles.

It is important to note that, the youth who has trained himself adequately to be fit for leadership is no longer a "youth" by virtue of the acquisitions, reflexes, and temperament. You are now in adulthood, matured and ready to handle matured issues of life as servant of the people. At this stage, to you, age is just a number. You have learnt 'to wash your hands well enough to dine with the elders', as we say in my village.

The adults referred to here, is not the chronological adult with grey hair but those people called Elders. Those people who have distinguished themselves with selflessness, honesty and dedication to the society. Those who have offered something back to society and humanity. So as a requirement, the youth is required to follow the steps of these statesmen, learn and become leaders in the various endeavours of the society.

Be a Peace Maker and Enforcer of It

Peace is an essential commodity for every society to develop and achieve its collective goals. Peace ensures continuity of thought and development. It entrenches trust, detests acrimony, mistrust, bitterness and any act that threatens harmonious co-existence among citizens. The price of peace is immeasurable. We can only have a glimpse of its absence if we consider the ruins in Somalia, North Eastern DR Congo, Sierra Leone, Liberia, and Kosovo, The United Sates, Berlin, France and other parts of Europe after their wars and disturbances.

The human and infrastructural costs are huge; the cost of lost values, the bitterness sown and embedded seeds of hate have been inconceivable as witnessed in trouble spots and war torn countries. It is important for you to ensure that, the foundations of our nation, one of which is peace is not shaken. It is because, this *peace* serves as the ligaments which values trust, love, commitment, hard work, rewards, and communality have been tied up to link us together. You have a role to protect the peace of the society at whatever cost. Sometimes some of you are the instruments of violence and many other chaotic events. Additionally, you must not only abstain from being used as instruments of violence and destruction, you must within your means prevent them.

The irony is that, the youth who are being used for these acts are the biggest losers. You lose opportunities to go to school, learn a trade, build a prosperous society, and achieve your dreams.

In line with the quest for peace and securing the same, you have a national duty to speak out against it, expose any violent undercurrents, shun violence and make deliberate and conscious efforts to fight against any act or group of people whose interest threatens the peace of the society. This is one of your duties which directly benefit you in the immediate and long terms.

You should not hesitate about this struggle to ensure peace in the society. It calls for boldness and you must rise to it. It calls for collective actions which require that individuals and groups should join your resources through advocacy, clubs and volunteerism to ensure that the peace of the society is always paramount.

You ought to have an orientation of mind, views and aspirations in order to muster the courage to perform this important role. You need the independence of mind to stave off bad influences from the status quo which is always whispering to you that, 'it can never be done in the motherland'.

In adding to this, you would need an ability to critically evaluate counsel with a dint of discernment to be able to identify the soft voices urging you not to embrace the ventures of violence which would later become scars on our conscience and blunt your future.

Stepping Away from Drugs and joining the fight Against It

There is no doubt about the harm caused by drugs. Its effects on you are devastating, yet as easily as possible many of you are enticed and led astray. Drugs steal your dreams, potentials and render you unworthy in the society. Considering the immense responsibility and trust on your shoulders, it is important for you to avoid drugs so as to avail your potentials and resources to the development of the nation. Do not be deceived by the short term deceptive benefits of drugs. Doctors, inventors and whatever class of professionals required for national goals, evolves from your ranks. For this reason, it is an issue of national duty, that you do not waste your potential on drugs. Thus staying away from drugs is a national responsibility. The nation needs you healthy. Furthermore, you should not only stay away from drugs, you must speak against it, expose those behind its supply and distribution and extend a hand to those caught in it.

Your Roles in fighting Crime, Delinquency and Hooliganism

Crime, delinquency and hooliganism are challenges you have to confront and abstain from. One of the ways for you to fight crime is to stay away from it and not to experiment with it.

Do not hang out with drug users and do not be carried away by curiosity. If you could stay away or make a decision to stay away from crime and violence, your bright minds could be made available for national development.

Staying away from crime in many instances would not be enough. Individuals and Youth groups ought to voice the negatives of crime in a concerted and sustained manner. In this respect, youth groups should, by way of advocacy and education, attempt to influence policy makers in making provisions for the vulnerable youth in this direction. Institutional capacity of the National Union of Students, Union of Polytechnic Students, Medical Students Association, Teacher Trainees Association and other Youth groups should be improved to help you offer constructive contributions towards the containment of juvenile crime within their fold and beyond.

You are Agents of Change and Innovation

You have the duty to serve as agents of change. The responsibility of bringing in new ideas, innovations, and new areas of development to meet national goals equally rest with you. Suffice to say, of course, there should be a youth policy to give direction and create the necessary environment. Your energy and the opportunity offered by information technology afford you opportunities to increase your knowledge in key areas, conduct research, break new grounds, create new opportunities and serve as a bank for new areas of development to meet national goals.

Changes are at a point in time needed. As a society, we are at such a time, when the environment has weak institutions to support productive and progressive youth development. When the status quo becomes too strong and chokes fresh ideas, direction, freedom of thought, then there is the need for a change. When the status quo does not inspire, and has thus become the instrument of the few privileged people then there is the need for an attempt to transform the system in a way to provide equal opportunities for all. When the status quo does not allow merit to prevail, so that the son or daughter of the peasant farmer can have chance of a better future in the Motherland as the child of the rich, then there should be the need for a new system that would cater for all who dream and sacrifice for their dreams.

You have a key role in history, and by nature, and desire to serve as change agents in restoring the environment to a level where a fair and (or) acceptable field would be created.

The ideas for transformation, the activism for change, the drive and desire for rebuilding an environment to suit you should come from you. Not all of you but those of you whose upward climb has been seriously hampered not because you are not qualified, but because you have no lineage and strings to pull down opportunities for you. You are the hungry. You are those who see your dreams fading and disappointments driving you to madness. The numerous hurdles along your path upset you.

You should seek this reform through youth groups, political activism, and proposal representation to state, international bodies and non-governmental organisations and not along unguided paths, like violent demonstration, rioting, and vandalism.

The thrust of the argument here is that, you have to make the decision to pursue new ideas, new directions with their unique challenges and uncertainties through the renewal of your minds. This would come with a huge price. This is an appeal as well as a moral call.

You are supposed to Have Dreams and Ambitions

It is your absolute duty to dream and dream big. It is your responsibility to dream to be successful and to have drive and purpose in life. Being a member of this society comes with responsibilities and for you, there is no running from it even though without the slightest of doubt, this society has not or is not giving you enough opportunities.

You must be driven by an ambition and a desire to make an imprint on your family, generation and society. Arguments have been earlier made against baseless dreams and wishes. The urge here is that, you have to live for a purpose. This is not a command. It is a requirement for building a successful society.

Great nations are defined by the dreams and achievements of its citizens. Without big dreamers and visionaries, it would be difficult to make giant strides in achievements and innovation. The natural resources of a nation and favourable geographic factors would serve that nation no purpose towards great achievements if they are not matched and motivated by a great sense of purpose, drive and ambition.

Rarely can a single dream unilaterally lift a society in all spheres of endeavour and needs. It is the collective dreams of all which would ignite the fire of inspiration and lead the society to a better place. In this spirit, you are urged to have a unique sense of direction, focus and vision, which would place you in a place of usefulness among your peers and the society.

It is important for you to bear in mind that, it is your duty to have dreams, which would be uplifting to the nation. You cannot just live and go around without any sense of purpose, direction and motivation in this life. The nation requires you to harness your resources to dream and work hard to achieve those dreams.

The environment created might not be friendly, yet it is required of you to bear that, the nation needs you to lift it up by having vision, dreams and sense of purpose.

You Are Required to Be Your Own Person

You must endeavour to be your own person by carrying your own 'burden'. In this light, you should be genuine and independent in thought and must be prepared to take responsibility for your actions. You must neither be a burden to your families, friends nor to society.

Thinking Critically and Using Your Mental Power

It is important for you to acknowledge that, it is your duty to think critically in order to help in solving complex problems facing you and the society. Furthermore, you owe it to yourself and the society to think outside the box in order to overcome dogmas. You must challenge and or analyse conventions at every stage of your life. Do not be intimidated by awe of personalities and institutions. You should only be humbled by superior wisdom. You owe the society this much.

If you fail to think and challenge conventions and the status quo, you would lose your path and with it your dreams. Often, most of you are being held back by dogmas, half truth and in some cases absolute lies. These inhibit any dream to reach new heights. Do not be afraid. Use your mind, which is a powerful weapon in overcoming any challenge you would face in life. Search for that mental power and move ahead towards light to free yourself. If you fail to think and analyse issues, you are not only failing yourself but the society as well.

CHAPTER 3

THE STATUS QUO: THE WAY THINGS ARE TODAY

'If there is dissatisfaction with the status quo, good. If there is ferment, so much the better. If there is restlessness, I am pleased. Then let there be ideas, and hard thought, and hard work. If man feels small, let man make himself bigger.'

Hubert H. Humphrey (1911-1978); 38th US Vice President under Lyndon B. Johnson (1965-1969) And Senator, 1949-64; 1971-1978

You are in an uncertain and volatile society which has almost lost the code: honour, dignity and self-respect. You are situated in a society of perpetual indiscipline, recklessness and low mindedness. Neither is there a strengthened institution with effective running programmes to sustain nor grow you into a useful citizen. Many of you are rowing in an environment of anarchy. You have no sense of order and procedure.

You are growing in a society where greed, wickedness, lies, deceit, fear and doubt are so common that, you may have come to accept them as part of the 'virtues' of life. These vices are so daunting that, some of you have been suppressed into 'no-search' of ways to escape from this net of weakness. Rather, many of you are adjusting to conforming to them.

Persons you have come to know and respect as heroes and role models are constantly being exposed of their greed, selfishness and lack of dignity by the day. Whatever institution you consider, people are being exposed daily for graft, greed, sycophancy, and lies.

44

Many among the Clergy, Chieftaincy, Police, Academia, and Politicians have largely, fallen from grace.

You have few or no heroes at all. You have equally few role models. It is a society of the *old-bad-ways*. A society of self -seeking, self-righteous individuals whose hold on power, be it economic, political or cultural, has not brought prosperity to all but to themselves and a very few. As a result, many of you have resigned to live undignified lives: laziness, indiscipline, with little hope, ambition and without leaders.

Every society has the obligation to create the right environment that meets the aspirations of her youth: provides and secures their happiness not through lies and misinformation, rather through concrete programmes and achievements. The youth needs the environment to pursue their aspirations and opportunities to develop and achieve goals they have or would set for themselves.

Additionally, they need such an environment not only to develop themselves but to uphold and sustain our values and our societies as a nation. They need to develop to gain the requisite skills, knowledge, attitudes and temperament which are unique to the environment, which they so wish to protect. The protection of the environment could not be said to be the sole prerogative of the youth. This is a basic fact. The crux of the issue here is that, the size and potentials of the youth make them useful for this and many key roles in the society.

It is only within a conducive environment that the youth has any hope of achieving his dreams. The right environment is key to the proper development of the youth and sustainability of the society, considering the responsibilities the society expects them to bear. And so, it is important to fight for such an environment.

The Need for Progressive Ideas

The status quo must change to make way for progressive ideas, new knowledge and new attitudes which reflect on the requirements of modern times. The current society has little hope for any of you with BIG dreams. It neither inspires nor gives space for you to plan and pursue lifelong dreams. It is suited for the mediocre by turning a large number of you into gossips, bootlickers, sycophants and little minds. Many of you live by the hour on mediocrity and die in large numbers by the minutes for nothing.

The environment is fraught with frustrations, hardships and acrimony so much that, many of you have been broken up. Others have taken solace in drugs, and delinquent behaviour. Counselling services have broken down in towns and cities, with some few exceptions in some villages, conducted by Queen Mothers and Elders and the few good parents out there. Social services no longer exist beyond signboards and policy papers. There is nothing more costly to a nation, than whole generations of young persons passing through life without proper education, skills, dreams and ambitions.

Do not let politicians tell you what they have for you. Inform them what you need from them. Share your thoughts with them.

Houses of God Could Do Better for You

In many houses of God, the only area counselling services have a semblance of existence is in marriages where the pastor and or church elders would constitute a board to counsel the would-be husband and wife. In the larger society, you have few places to turn to for professional advice. Counselling services at Social Welfare centres are inactive for lack of capacity and resources.

It is not worth at any price to allow such a vacuum to exist in the society. If we fail to address this vacuum, we allow the youth to seek for their own solutions to their challenges. In such a situation, they become vulnerable to many excesses. This would worsen an already bad situation. It is prudent for the religious groups to step up their counselling services for the youth. This is partly because of their ability to cut across traditional and cultural lines.

Where Do You Turn to for guidance?

There is a nagging question about who should fill the vacuum so created by the failed state institutions. Is it the Churches, Muslims, Traditional Authorities or Civil Society? There is no doubt that, this vacuum ought to be filled. In the absence of active counselling services in the home and society, you are left on your own and in this environment with huge challenges; only a few could survive. Some of you are either snatched as tools of violence, prostitution, armed robbery and as delinquents or left to waste on drugs and other vices.

A society with no adequate support services for its youth is inhibiting their development. The situation is even more precarious when the status of homes these days are thrown into the equation. With family breakups, single mothers and absentee fathers, you are most vulnerable.

In the light of this, many of you are exposed to so many temptations and challenges you cannot overcome. After school opportunities for many of you are also non-existent. The lack of adequate structures such as counselling centres, public library facilities, and recreational centres to cater for you have rendered you handicapped considering your complicated modern roles in nation building.

This is the environment as it is today. This environment cannot be said to be able to support any fruitful youth development programmes. It does not inspire. It does not provide much sense of hope or purposefulness. Institutions are weak. The political will for long term programmes is also weak.

The neglect of the youth by the society is standard and has been barely challenged. The society has gone unchecked, and political leadership who have been the biggest culprits for a long time have not shown the political will to challenge this state of affairs. In Ghana, a comprehensive and coordinated youth policy to serve as a road map for youth development has barely been passed by Parliament after twenty (20) years. In March 2010, a large section of Zimbabwean youth rose up to challenge a defective youth policy drafted in 2000 and adopted in 2004. According to the youth leaders, the policy 'lacked a comprehensive and multi-sectoral approach to its implementation'. Further, the policy ever since has remained 'only on paper', since no concrete action has been taken to implement the document. Similar stories abound across the continent.

Even in situations where youth policies have been passed, implementation has become problematic.

(*I have considered the question of youth policy and programmes in my book: "The African Youth Question")*

Threat from Powerful People

The society is filled with financial, political and social godfathers who now control the machinery of production, economic and political powers and whatever route you need to pursue your dreams. More and more, it seems you cannot pursue much serious business venture without their approval. They can say who, what and when it is supposed to be done. Their word is 'final' and sometimes, political leadership cannot challenge them.

These demagogues and short sighted persons define and control the environment and in their greed, ruthlessness, and selfishness, they have designed the environment to suit them or their preferred outlets. There is no fairness in their dealings. Their goal is their interest. They are always quick to nib any threat or perceived threat in the bud. Such is the reality that, it is difficult to urge you to dream or pursue any meaningful venture outside their influences.

The grasp of these godfathers could be better understood when one considers the reach of their interest in commerce, politics and society. They have the power to overturn laws passed by the representative of the people. They control government agenda and with their media allies, sway public opinion. In an environment where the public is more gullible, the media not critical, and our value system nose diving, it is not at all difficult for such culture to flourish.

You Will Win The Fight

You should not lose hope. Have hope in our human nature. Take strength in your *will*. The human *will* combined with thought and proper actions becomes a force which can surmount any obstacle. You should believe and continue to develop your dreams. Above all, have hope in the transformational power of time. Time brings healing. Time strengthens. Time brings change. It brings freedom. Time chooses and if your dreams are right, communal, and your heart is pure, you would be blessed with the opportunity to see your dreams through for the good of the poor, the hopeless, the weak and those who seek only their daily bread.

The other window is that, the strength of these men would not wage war forever. Eventually, their strength will fade with age or time and give way to change. You only have to refuse to join them. Then time would shed light on their legacies. At those moments, you would only remember them for who they really were. Their ill-amassed wealth of today would count for nothing.

You shall really see them as little men, selfish and short sighted. Live your dreams and hold on to them. The hurricane you see today, would not last forever. Whatever they destroy, time would restore. Time brings healing, growth and restoration.

Greed, as used here, implies an insatiable appetite for material wealth beyond what is really necessary. They are never satisfied. They crave for more and more. They lack contentment. They have no sense of balance. The wealth or whatever they seek might not mean anything to them, yet they gather beyond the point of madness. They have more than they need in three life-times. What they seek has become a nuisance to them, yet they never seem to ignore their gluttony. They take from everyone: the poor, needy and even among themselves.

By selfishness, these people seek their own and only interests. What they have is never shared, distributed, loaned and or made available to anyone. They live for themselves and their own interest at any cost. Even their generosity is a burden to those who benefit from them.

The reality is that, by ruthlessness and by all means at their disposable, they would eliminate anything in their way. When it comes to their interest, they show no reason; they do not second guess their proposed actions. They are prepared to destroy lives unnecessarily to protect their interests.

Remember That Your Big dreams May not Be Their Priority

The power structure may not necessarily care about your big dreams, your uplift and inspirations. Whereas people built nations and business empires from very little, the elites of our society have not only failed to build upon that which was left to them by the noble section of that first generation which secured our political independence. Sadly, the elite of today have almost destroyed the very foundation which was left to them to preserve for you. More disturbingly, they are building nothing in place of what they have squandered.

The Examples of Our Founding Fathers

The issue is not only the attempted spread of services and building of institutions by many of our founding fathers but their commitment, to a large extent, to the future.

They could have lived beyond comfort as it is now. But not them; they sacrificed something for today. They were not a perfect generation as no generation would ever be. They left footprints for the present. They built universities, laid foundation for science and technology, built dams, whole cities and townships, road infrastructure, teaching hospitals, ministerial infrastructures, and above all a dream for a better future and a prosperous nation; a nation where the present generation sacrifices for the next and prepares for the future. A nation where it would not be regarded as a luxury to have three square meals, buy a house or own a car.

Many of Our Modern Leaders Are Different

The present is so different. Many of your national leadership are so corrupt and indifferent. The combination of greed, selfishness, gluttony and moral decadence in a single political body makes them really threatening to the health of the environment and any youth outside their circles. They are indeed a threat to the building of any institution and programme that would tend to change the status quo. These forces fight against reform and as such, all necessary force is needed to be exerted by your leadership and society to defeat them if we are to build a society better for all. In the light of this, you ought to urge your leadership to be open, accountable and visionary enough to point to the right direction. On the other hand, the society must hold leadership accountable to their promises, actions and negligence.

"I'm not interested in preserving the status quo; I want to overthrow it."

Niccolò di Bernardo dei Machiavelli: (3rd May 1469 – 21st June 1527) An Italian Historian, Philosopher, Humanist, and Writer based in Florence during the Renaissance: The Author of 'The Prince'

You Need Structures and Institutions to replace godfathers

The success story of our traditional societies has been the fact that, they are all based on strong institutions. These institutions, chieftaincy, marriage, and family, have been the foundation of all our societies. In the wisdom of our fathers, they protected, and nurtured them and as they did, our societies grew and became stronger. Institutions became the guiding blocks of the societies as well as the custodian of our collective wisdom.

In this wisdom, in the modern society, we need to create and support institutions. As these institutions grow and mature, they would replace personalities. These institutions would oversee the nation and make it better for all. So instead of mentioning names of strong personalities, we would mention values such as honesty, discipline, humility, hard work and generosity and institutions such as the Department of Social Welfare, Youth Authority, the Trade Ministry and other relevant institutions. Strongmen create imbalance within the society. They prevent the society from creating and maintaining order. Agreeably, without order we can neither live freely nor protect the weak and the vulnerable.

These faceless forces creating imbalance in the society are not alone in advocating their agenda. Their resources buy them political influence and untouchable social status. They have long arms and their reach is so deep that, it takes a lot to identify let alone confront them. They have created a customized environment, which is also private in nature. This environment is created by a few and it is now being controlled by an even smaller number. That is, the path to the few jobs are controlled by few and they line them up for the few who are connected to them; maybe nephews, nieces, children and sycophants. The standard is not on merit but on affiliation, lineage and perceived loyalty or the regard for something done some time ago. This is the nature of your environment as you set out to pursue your dreams.

We are in an environment where mediocrity is preferred over excellence; greed over contentment; cheapness over quality, and sycophants are preferred over critics and the level headed. These have been the evil destroying our society by preventing it from being progressive.

It is essential for you to urge leadership and opinion leaders to accommodate excellence and create space for it within the society. It is largely within an acceptable space that excellence, this essential value, can find room and fertile grounds to flourish. You must 'force' the society to create this space by rewarding excellence and other values in all endeavours of life:

business, entrepreneurship, academia, music, public service, religion, culture, advocacy, and related fields.

Furthermore, you must show a strong dislike for mediocrity in all endeavours of public and private lives by pointing them out and speaking against them.

You Are Matured To Play A Role In National Issues

There is no doubt that, you have a role to play in the transformation of the society. The roles you play come in various forms but to ensure your participation in the society, it is important you get involved in decision making and national issues.

By this way, you would consider yourselves as part of the society and also as stakeholders in the destiny and the attainment of our national aspirations.

As the situation stands today, in some countries, decisions are made without key inputs from you. It is not always a question of capacity on your part. Rather, it has become a culture for policy makers and political leadership to ignore you and create disjointed, outmoded and sometimes non-responsive policies to cater for your interest, albeit with good intentions.

With the surge in individual skills and development and the maturity the youth has shown in recent times, it is time for them to have a broader representation on national issues and on related programmes. The status quo says it is not possible to either involve you or accept your effective participation in decisions affecting you and the nation. Do not accept this position. Make it clear that, you are matured and capable.

You Must Take A Step Forward

Suffice to say, you should not expect change or greater participation to be handed over to you in a ceremony or as change of baton as in a relay race. There has to be a renewed vigour in charting a new and better course in participating in national development. The youth ought to show maturity, patriotism and innovation whilst respecting our values. On the other hand, the few ones who are now key players in society and national development must show greater commitment, hard work, honesty and quality in their entrusted endeavours. By these, they would prove to the society that, the youth is ready, capable and dependable.

It should be noted that, there are few areas the youth is involved though. In academic institutions, students are represented in Hall Councils, Junior Common Rooms (JCRs) and University Councils. For example, the youth is represented on the Ghana Education Trust fund (GET FUND). The Student Representative Council has representation on many school committees.

The Problem Of A Conservative Culture

Many of the challenges you are facing are also as a result of conservative traditions, and it is no longer a grand secret. Where the powers of state and society bear no remorse for denying you so much, then it behoves the society to rationally debate with the aim of establishing why the status quo should be maintained. By the youth, the reference is not the few who by virtue of blood or privilege are benefitting from the society. Rather, we are looking at the masses of you who are without connections and voices in high places. Those of you whose only capital is your hard earned skills, academic certificate and drive. You are the silent majority. These masses are only asking for your stake in the society, a descent job, opportunities and a dignified life in the motherland. An opportunity to live and work in the motherland with dignity and commanding respect as an American, a Chinese, or a Brazilian would in their native lands.

Lack of Supportive Social and Physical Environment

Does the current environment, physical and social, support development? This is a question I came across as I gathered materials for this book. What you see around you, what you experience and hear are issues at variance to the core values you have been taught to believe in and practice in basic school literature, folklore and fireside stories. Any time you hear the enormous issues of corruption, graft and embezzlement, the moral barometer is lowered further. Any time you see an old age man 'haunt' some of your friends, you redefine decency. Anytime you hear of the duplicity of Chiefs in violence, you question the necessity of the chieftaincy institution in modern times.

These flawed character traits, injustices and wrongful acts being committed by the leaders of society, industry, culture and politics are being forced upon you by the environment which these characters have created. As you experience injustice and witness the imbalances within the society, you are confused as to who you are, what to believe in and what you can do. You are thrown into confusion and whatever seed of light sowed in you comes to risk. By this, many a generation of you have been destroyed or lost to the course of honesty, freedom and dignity.

Often, some of you dishonour yourselves to fit into that society which has been created through all manner of habits and characters. This is partly as a result of personal weakness; but most are as a result of your inability to overcome hurdles in the environment, even as, 'we must impress upon (you) that, (you) would face difficulties' and as such, you must be prepared to make sacrifices and bear pains along the way.

It is important to demand from the society examples for you to follow before you lose the future. It is important to forcefully point out to leaders that, your future is non-negotiable.

You Need Social Protection

Protections within the environment are necessary for your development. You need a physical and social environment that promotes good health and offers protection from physical harm. You need an environment providing a means to a sustainable and dignified livelihood. You need a society that protects you from shocks, unemployment, diseases and is free from violence and rough neighbourhoods. That is an environment, which exudes values worth emulating and dedicating one's life to.

Protection does not only mean physical concerns. The bigger issue is to protect your minds and souls from unhelpful foreign cultures and voices. This means that sometimes you need guidance as to what to read and watch as well as what you should do with your lives and issues worth pursuing in this life.

Relative to these are two other issues. The first has to do with saving your fresh minds, and the second is saving those of you who have fallen to an inferiority complex and have thus embraced defeat as the larger part of their life. Require from the society to redeem those of you who have been stolen by fear and inferiority. You must help to rebuild them to believe in themselves, stand up among their peers and tell them that, they are as good as an the American, British, Japanese, Indian or Chinese youth.

There is the need for you to acknowledge that, in a competitive world, your confidence and outlook is as good as your Bachelor of Science (BSc), Master of Arts (MA), or Master of Business Administration (MBA). Without self belief, you are like any other person irrespective of your training and academic qualifications. But you cannot succeed by being like any other person. You have to be unique, confident, bold and competitive.

Without conscious efforts to achieve this end, no amount of academic education would recover your situation. You have to be confident again as your peers were in the days of struggle for political independence when they saw themselves as equal to any of their peers around the world; at a time when they believed they had a calling and a mission in the future of their nations.

Dilemma Of The Society

The society needs to be a Mother for the youth. At the same instance, the society ought to give you options and allow you to make choices. There is a dilemma here. If we allow you to make independent choices, there is the fear that, you would make wrong choices and if we prevent you from making life's choices, we stifle your growth and maturity. That fear seems to be a stranglehold on any bold attempt to free you. That is to say, the fear of your failure to balance between how much you ought to know and failure to make right choices on your own tempts the society to prevent you from developing.

Between fear of making wrong choices and learning new knowledge which leads to challenging exposures, I would beg to urge for a choice of the latter. There could be no justification for the restriction of knowledge you could harness. Independence of thought and choices are necessary elements in growth and maturity. Choices and their consequences are necessary for learning. What you need to be reminded of is that, every decision has consequences. As such, you should be prepared to bear the consequences of your decisions without shifting blame.

The youth should not be left alone in making certain choices all alone by themselves though. Issues with dire consequences which are likely to affect you all your life should have an input from the parent or elders. Thus, in the issues of marriage, career choices, and other major decisions of life, parents need to make strong input to make sure that you get your options right. Yet, the final decision in all matters should be left to you though. You alone would be responsible for your decisions.

You May Be Part Of The Problem

Every one of you faces a myriad of challenges. Some of these challenges are unquestionably as a result of the environment; but obviously, quite a number of them are as a result of the actions, inactions and choices you make. At this stage, you are beyond assigning of blame and sharing of the same.

It is time to stand up and be noticed. Not by wealth of money or boasts of certificates, but by your contributions to the society. It is a time to own up to your choices and responsibilities. Make a decision not to be part of the problem. Decide to be of use and help to solve the daunting challenges facing your generation. Do not join the ranks of the greedy fathers for their short term pleasures. Do not be enticed by their praises, financial conveyances, perks and empty luxury. Do not be part of that godless team of saboteurs. You are better than that. You are hungry, unemployed and as such tempted. Yet stay the course and be a better young person. They would come to you with so much 'comfort' but stay true to the dreams of a prosperous Africa.

You Need Unity Among Your Ranks

Integration among and between you and the larger society is proving to be a growing future challenge facing the nation. On many University campuses today, you are split among ethnic unions. There is the Asante Student Union, Hausa Fraternity, Xhosa Student Union, Zululand, among other unions. Hitherto, the popular craze on campuses was Literary Clubs and Debating Associations.

The concern is that, literary clubs are fading out whilst ethnic groups on campuses are on the ascendency. Whereas literary clubs sharpened your critical thinking and built a stronger mind, these ethnic sectarianism attacks the very heart of the concept of nationhood and unity among you. This is not to say, fading of literary clubs are as a result of ethnic groups. The primary concern is that, you see yourselves more as ethnic entities rather than as units of intellectuals and beacons of light and development for the nation. Consider yourselves as more of a nation and less of an Asante or Wala or a Yoruba. It is within this framework that we can be sure of forging ahead with a common interest in trust, unity, and grace collectively.

The Saga Of Delinquency

Delinquency has become an established culture among your ranks, with recent cult dimensions. Crime is a popular culture not only in sprouting slums, low earning communities and ghettoes but also in high class communities. Drugs, rioting and prostitution under the disguise of such name as escorts, office services, fixers and 'job applicants' have come to be associated with your generation.

The price you are paying for living in a society such as this one is your future.

Delinquents are often disregarded by society. They are seen to be of no use to the society, be it economic, social or moral. We see them in the mirror of our biases and indifference and conclude that, they are a waste to the society; people who could make no substantial contribution to the society.

Those of you in disadvantaged communities and those in the challenging environments have been stereotyped as a burden on society. Indeed, stereotyping is erroneous. The serious consequence of stereotyping is that, it puts walls between you and thus prevents many of you from progressing beyond your societies.

The successful youth we see around us as role models could have ended up on their side of the society. Our environment, negligence and lack of supportive measures end up denying most of you the opportunities required to be meaningful citizens.

Delinquents require the opportunity to get out of their present situation. Delinquents require rehabilitation, as we strive as a society to ensure that the fertile grounds which create them are defeated.

Walls Within the Society

As it is, the society has created walls along poverty and wealth lines, which prevent certain classes of youth from pursuing lofty dreams. They are inhibited by poverty and lack of employable skills. So, many of you are being left behind. Indeed, large parts of your generation are being left behind in education, skills training and in the pursuit of lofty dreams.

Economic, social and environmental conditions have created artificial walls among you. The resultant imbalances among the various youth groups by virtue of their disadvantaged situation would create conflict in the society. This conflict is a nagging challenge to the society. It may not be latent for long. It would not be a secret kept by a few for long. It would be a national challenge to confront this issue at the budding stage before it tears the future apart.

Correctional Institutions May Not Be Enough

It is important to note that, the case of delinquents is unique and requires unique solutions. Thus, lodging delinquents into institutions where the balance among skills, academic knowledge and moral values are not even is problematic. Balances among various elements of training are necessary to support the special needs of the delinquent, the delusional and the broken young persons in society.

In the light of this, it is important for the right efforts to be made and sustained. It is a matter of fact that, these delinquents would require the necessary skills inherent in tapping into the opportunities available in the society. They are not outcasts. The society should neither treat them so nor leave them to fate.

The existing delinquency correctional institutions are neither right nor apt. They have become grounds for further degradation and rot. Young persons 'go in' and 'come out' worse. These institutions have lost their souls and purpose. While they retain some level of usefulness, it is worth stating that, it is difficult to argue for its worth in their current state of stagnation and neglect. Their absence may leave delinquents worse though. It behoves youth leaders to charge political leadership to commit adequate resources to reforming correctional centres.

If the society succeeds, even limitedly, in correcting the delinquent youth, which we should, all stand to achieve a lot from these youths making use of their talents and energies to contribute to the dream; the dream of a prosperous nation, where no youth is left behind. A society abundant in opportunities where there would be no limit to your rise.

Let us acknowledge that, even though the task would be tough, the fruits stand to be great and, therefore, let the society not only look at the economic cost in the present economic situation, but also look at the socioeconomic benefits we are to gain from reformed delinquents and deviants.

If they fail and or fall behind, the society loses. The society does not only lose from the fact that bright minds might have been lost, but of equal importance is the fact that, these delinquents, eventually turn out to be the thieves, gangsters, and armed robbers who would pose as threats to our scarce resources. Politicians owe this much to you. Remember that, until you act in a determined and concerted manner, there would be no meaningful action on the part of politicians in this direction.

We cannot and should not take this as a gamble. Let this society be a place for all. Let the society be a mother caring for all her children. This nation should be a society where no youth is left behind.

Issues Of Morality In An Internet Age

The issues of morality and cultural bearing are important. Our society, by virtue of our ethnic grouping, has numerous moral codes. This notwithstanding, certain codes are widely accepted. These include, severally; volunteerism, discipline, humility, maturity, learning, communality, teamwork, level headedness, generosity, hard work, respect for life and dignity. This moral code has fast degenerated. Transition into the internet age – social networking, search engines and chat rooms—has been too fast for the society and made the act the more difficult. With no explicit governance protocols in place, among others, the internet age has left many of you gliding badly in unchartered areas with little to guide you.

Furthermore, structural weaknesses within the National Youth Institutions coupled with the stagnation of the National Commission on Culture and The Ministry of Youth and Sports make it the more difficult for the society to guide the youth in making use of this wonderful age.

CHAPTER 4

THE STRUGGLE BETWEEN YOUR NEW IDEAS AND OLD IDEAS

'The youth feels this environment is built against their interests and largely, they are willing to wage war by any means available to them for their selfish comfort and, second, for the preservation of the society. He may be right. He may be wrong. Whatever it is, the environment is questionable and unsuited for preparing the youth for this century.'

Unknown

The struggle between the old and the new is as old as time itself. This is not a struggle between age and number. It is a struggle between new ideas, new knowledge and new ways on one hand and the existing beliefs on the other. It has been waged for a long time with, sometimes, bloody conclusion. It should be stressed that, "you", as denoted in this context does not refer to the fifteen year old young man only. "You" as used here, also refers to innovations, which ought to be ushered in to displace, reform or complement the current order for the purposes of moving the dynamics of progress in the direction required for creating a viable and sustainable environment.

As per your perspective, outlook and ideas and not by age, you are seen to be at logger heads with the outmoded ways of doing things.

You challenge the traditional ways not only because they do not favour you, but also because you see them as outmoded and cumbersome; thus something ought to be done to bring in the new society to make things better, efficient and deliver the promise of a better life for all. Yet, you are likely to face challenges. Change does not come on a silver platter.

It is worth stating though that, as long as the object is to create a better environment, it is prudent for the suspicion and brute resistance to make way for accommodation and tolerance in the hope of building a better environment for your future. But note that, reforms are never readily accepted.

This usual struggle has naturally created disorder and stress. The old are afraid of losing their comfort and interests and you are afraid of the status quo.

In the light of this, a long battle is being waged perpetually between these forces. Reform does not come easily. Transformation of society has always been met with resistance. But as the battle wages on, it is my hope that, reforms wins for the better.

Obviously, for the purposes of self interests and other latent reasons, the old has always viewed any act by you with suspicion. This suspicion and apprehension have largely influenced their decisions, action and inactions. This has largely resulted in unpleasant, petty and rush actions which do not serve the interests of both you and the larger society.

Use Of Violence Is Unacceptable

On the other hand, it has been long held that, on most occasions the youth has failed to use legitimate laid down means in pursuing your means of change; violence, radicalism, rioting, hooliganism, are but a few of the means which have characterised your pursuit for change and a better environment.

A minority school of thought among you though believes that, resorting to violence is justified in situations where all avenues of peaceful redress are deliberately blocked. The employment of these methods is problematic and you cannot be said to be right with these methods even as you pursue lofty goals. There is no doubt that, the pursuit of new goals sometimes requires unconventional means, but deliberate and outright violence as a tool is unacceptable.

The issue of the struggle between you and the old, new ideas versus the status quo, heroes and villains is sometimes underestimated and overestimated. On one hand, the old seeks to keep, nourish and grow the status quo whereas you, in seeking answers to your poor situation seek to alter so many things including the status quo, in the hope of a better environment. Sometimes you might not know the eventual outcome. To you, having demonised the status quo, you blindly hope that a new system would be better. With this urge, you set out for reforms in rage and drive.

Sometimes, it is important to pause to ask some basic questions. Is the status quo bias against you? Are you disadvantaged because of the status quo with its persistent failures and weaknesses, or you are failing as a result of your own laziness, lack of commitment and skills to tap into the opportunities in the environment or lack of vision?

Suffice to say, one of the underlining issues at the core of this struggle to both the old and new is one of survival. The former looking to keep interests which he feels would secure his survival in the society and you, seeking to alter the status quo to reflect part of your vision for survival and a better future.

If we have a reasonably fair order then we would be at ease to say that, issues would resolve by themselves and many interests would be met.

On the other hand, because we have a bias order in place, the beneficiaries of this order fear that with the erosion of the status quo, the new order would alter the current to their disadvantage. Or throw them in uncertain waters of fear, anxiety and apprehension which the environment they have created has forced upon the masses for so long. For this reason, among others, both you and the old view each other with suspicion and thus wage mental, physical and latent wars to outwit each other.

You have usually interpreted your actions as a mark of liberation whereas the old have seen their course as a mark of preservation; after all, they are the custodians of traditions, values and wisdom, which have come to define the society.

Of these battles, in the final event, the older conventionally loses. This is not a defeat as in wars of guns; rather it is giving in to new ideas and innovation albeit reluctantly. The final price has always been won by the new order with its new ideas and promise. It is on this platform that the war should be waged. And upon these goals we witness the often chaotic situations on your campuses, streets and public places.

Where Your Fight Normally Begins

The fight for reforms is sometimes neither seen nor even heard loudly. It is sometimes a whisper, murmured at the lecture hall; in the commuter buses; at the marketplace; or even in the bathroom; in the ghettos; at the backhouses and sometimes in the heat of the sun around the traffic lights selling pineapples, plantain chips, pens, dog chains and skipping ropes.

The Wise and Successful Youth

There is the need though to distinguish between the impulsive and often the arrogant all-knowing among you, who cares nothing about the dynamics or the wisdom in the way things are done. Those of you who, by virtue of your Bachelor of Arts Certificates, Master of Science Certificates and Doctor of Philosophy academic qualification, have lost all sense of balance and claim the real world to be at your feet.

Those of you mentioned here in the struggle exclude the misguided class. This is about the humble among you who are frustrated by backwardness and wishes to help in building a better society. I refer to those of you who have acquired the wisdom to manage your academic and skilled knowledge and are capable of managing what you seek, are seeking or would ever seek.

CHAPTER 5

WHAT YOU SHOULD SEEK FROM THE SOCIETY

*"The Youth should be given a chance to take an
active part in the decision-making of local, national
and global levels."*

Ban Ki-moon, United Nations Secretary-General,
1st January, 2007 – Date

There would be no argument about what you seek from the society if you point it out clearly. There is nothing so painful to see your talents unexplored, dreams slipping through your fingers through lack of opportunities, hopelessness and stupor while age, apathy, indifference and an uneven environment create the platform for only a few to excel.

What you should seek is a regenerative environment, which would help you to find your own paths to self-fulfilment but not at the expense of any member of the society. That is to say, a fulfilment which would help you to develop, create and (or) seek to pull yourselves upward within the society; a society which would help even the delinquent, drug addicts and those who have fallen behind to rise and pursue their aspirations freely and without fear of future failure.

Not to have a dream, drive and abilities is one thing, but to have them and yet be prevented by your environment and circumstances is not only painful but torturing. This usually drives many of you to tears and desperation.

At such a stage, some of you may fold because you find no hope in the environment. Others may turn to bitterness as a means of solace, which at some stage may drive you to attempt to tear the environment down. The tearful gasps at this stage, bursts of sorrow and hopelessness, may lead many a youth to dissociate yourselves from the society. I urge you to hang on. There would be a way out, as there always is.

At these moments, there is no longer any sense of eagerness to participate in the activities of the society and national development. You are at the end of the road where 'desire is no longer stirred' in you. Aspiration is at a standstill. The end is in sight.

Only a few of you may brace through these situations with a dint of hope that, your dreams would find a straw in the environment to hold on to because the drive in you for a secured future and dignified life is stronger than the challenges so created. This latter class among you is regrettably so few. They are either well bred by their homes to be immune to the environment or their maker has created them to overcome.

Strive painfully forward with hope, purpose, commitment and a sense of responsibility to achieving your dreams for a better future. Though difficult, such noble struggles as this rarely fail. This is a hope from history. Thus all who strive for success succeed, for 'fortune favours the bold' and the persistent, as God blesses the graceful, the humble, the hardworking and the good hearted.

Your Basic Needs

It is not far to identify your extrinsic needs in seeking to secure your identity and place in the society. These needs are clear and within the means of the society. It should be stated though that not all the idealistic wishes of the youth could be met by the society. By conventional wisdom, an enabling environment would create opportunities for as many of you who have acquired the needed skills as possible to succeed. Thus to sum up the struggle, it is urged that a better environment be created and sustained.

In my interaction with many of you and through observations, I have come to identify some of your basic needs which are realistic and achievable. These include a rich environment, jobs security, entrepreneurial support programmes and opportunities to pursue your dreams and aspirations in a dignified and respectful manner, either through education, sports, apprenticeship and skills training, commerce and public service.

What is required are smart policies, commitment and timely intervention on behalf of political leadership, stakeholders and the youth as a body. In this situation, what is necessary is for you as an individual or as a group to use your collective energies in achieving the goals common to you and useful to the society.

On many occasions, your leadership does not act with a deep sense of direction, purposefulness, focus, and the maturity required to be taken seriously by political leadership. Associations of national students' leadership and other blocks have all largely turned out to be appendages of political leadership for favours and related interests at the expense of the larger youth interest. The larger youth outside these student blocks are unorganised and expensive to reach.

In seeking for a rich environment, you should also look for accessible, quality and affordable education; training and internship opportunities; affordable source of funding for your business ideas; accessibility to information; access to ICT; freedom of expression; access to the knowledge and experiences of leaders of your respective fields of interests.

Furthermore, seek for participation in national development as a contribution to the building of society. The inclusiveness being sought should not be only on issues pertaining to your immediate personal needs, but also issues affecting your entire environment.

On the side of society, involving you in decision making processes and allowing you to contribute to the building of the same is paramount for harnessing your potentials and energies. Furthermore, it would also create the appropriate platform for you to learn and prepare yourselves for the higher and future task of sustaining this society and performing other duties the society may be generous to bestow on you now or later on in your lives.

There is the need to add that, in addressing your needs, a mention need to be made of a special kind among you. These are the physically and mentally challenged. It is worth noting that, they need the society to overcome their deficiencies for them to contribute to the national goal, since contribution to society is no longer reserved in physical abilities. Many an area are intellectual. It would be unfair and negligent to ignore them.

The society needs their potential and energy in one way or the other. Indeed, providing these afore-mentioned needs for you is obviously within the realm of the society. Every policy or programme put in place by government needs to address these issues and more. The call for opportunities, support and resources has been the long and arduous call of many of you for many years. Normally, you have made these calls through unconventional means with negative and dire consequences. The time has come for you to use constructive means.

Roles Of Parents Have Diminished

The roles of parents in the formation of your character are not central anymore. Formal education, peer pressure, mass media, social networks, game consoles and chat rooms have taken much control over your character formation and management.

The world is different now. Technology has changed the routes of information acquisition and in its wake, you are opened to a complex mix of cultures.

These new cultures present new challenges and hence new forms of guidance and advice. The truth is that, parents fail to adequately guide you in this maze. This failure to offer adequate advice in certain instances is not deliberate though. Many parents are unprepared to comprehend the thrust and complex dynamics of technologies and cultures, be it good or bad, available to you.

It is difficult to solve what you do not understand. Some of this information could not be provided by parents hence the temptation for you to look outside the family unit. That is the situation with most families.

The forceful thrust of technology and age difference has put a blinding veil between you and your parents. Not long ago, whistles and errand boys were used to woo girls out of the house. So parents would sit at the entrance of the house and keep watch. Not so these days. Text messages are more than enough. Even in villages where text messaging is not used, there seems to be subtle communication to outwit caring parents. Most of you have become so smart that, you outwit your parents right under their noses.

The internet and its knowledge quantum have made you a possessor of many things but less powerful in mastering and managing them. Largely, many of you are caught in youthful traps. The observation here is that, the parent or the old lady is no longer the sole source of knowledge and advice. This has diminished their roles and authority over your lives and thus, made you the more vulnerable.

The Generational Gap and Limited Knowledge

The pressures of work, poverty, and generational gap cannot be left out of our considerations. There is less time for the age-old custom of talking to you at dawn. Family meetings are no longer practiced.

Lack of information is not the only currency denying parents their rightful roles in your lives. Other issues are the depth and the variety of the information you need. An unfortunate situation is that, most parents are not up-to-date with time and the events of technology which has almost touched every face of our society.

CHAPTER 6

EFFECTS OF THE STRUGGLE FOR OPPORTUNITIES

'If you succumb to the temptation of using violence in the struggle, ...unborn generations will be the recipients of a long and desolate night of bitterness, and your chief legacy to the future will be an endless reign of meaningless chaos'.

Martin Luther King, Jr. (January 15th, 1929- April 4th, 1968) American Baptist Minister and Civil-Rights Leader.

The Path

The lure of wild dreams does not stand the test of time and reality. Neither does it appreciate tedious struggles of your mind and body nor the harsh realities of time and the environment. For you, to achieve your individual dreams may rest with each of you but for you to claim the dream of the nation rests with your combined efforts. Efforts which would spur the fires of desires eternally burning in you; fires which would burn pettiness, arrogance, laziness, and meanness and set you free to explore great heights and lofty dreams.

In fighting for reforms, you have a number of options. One option is to be part of one team and employ your strengths, so that the environment does not choke your dreams. You should not let the harsh environment around you discourage you. Let the dream be in your heart and mind and you would survive the storms of your life. By joining forces, you can see to it that, you are on the march to claim the nation's dream; a land of equal opportunities; land of abundance; a land where you can become whatever you aspire to be; the Land of Gold. This dream should not be defined by politicians or 'gods', but by you and you alone.

Urge the society that, if the businessman would pay his taxes; if the employer would treat workers right and invest in their development and equipment; if the worker would work hard to increase his output and stop stealing; if the journalist would not be bias and report with truthfulness and fairness; if priests would stand on the path of the truth and not be swayed by the 'lust of the eye' and of the flesh and 'the pride of this life'; if law enforcement officer would honour his codes, and the politician would stop plundering the resources of state, then the society could create and sustain a viable environment for you. And if we are able to overcome the temptations of our professions, then we shall say that, we are paying the price for our dreams.

Only Those with Skills Could Benefit from available Opportunities

It is worth noting that, if the much talked about environment is created, not all of you would benefit from it. It would take those of you who have acquired the basic skills and knowledge to benefit from it. It is in this light that it is important for each one of you to go beyond just dreams and writing down 'to-do list' and ask yourself what skills would be necessary for you to achieve your dreams within the environment.

There is no excuse to cry all day and year with the excuse of lack of opportunities. There is always an opportunity for you. Look for it. Ask for it and when you have found it, knock on doors to have them opened to you.

In creating the environment, each one of you has a responsibility, none lesser and none greater. Would you honour your part of the deal? Are you really doing your part?

Is that the best you can do? Are you working for the nation or you are spending more energy to keep in place the culture of corruption, meanness, laziness and mediocrity so established? The society awaits your inputs, and until you begin to do something right, we would not move forward as a nation.

The Way Forward

How then should you go about your change agent or pursue your dreams? Preparations and patience are necessary. There is a wide gap between awareness and reality. You ought to take time to read, study, ask questions and make extensive consultations.

Furthermore, you need a clear understanding of your environment and the demands of your dream. It is only after these that we can say that, you really understand the environment and are ready to engage in constructive activism to help in bringing about changes through dialogue, write-ups, procession, seminars and other means.

The Common Ground

The initial admonition towards a common ground is for you to acknowledge your inexperience in substantial matters of life and for the older generation to acknowledge on their part, their limitation with respect to your outlook, knowledge and energy in the context of current cultures and times as well as your early maturity periods.

Until these admissions are acknowledged, the common ground necessary for the nation to benefit from you would not be realised. In so saying, both you and older generations have merits, strengths and weaknesses. As such, there is the need for sober acknowledgement of the capacities and flaws of each.

Suffice to say, there is no question that each of you is trying to build and sustain a healthy environment. Both might believe in the same goal despite the fact that each has different needs within the goals.

CHAPTER 7

ARE YOU REALLY MATURED TO CONTRIBUTE TO NATIONAL DEVELOPMENT?

'The fact of life is that, no one would give leadership position to the youth because the youth so wish for it. It (change) is never easy. You would have to work for it. You would have to earn it. You would have to show maturity and a wealth of experience which would make you capable of managing the office you are vying for'.

J. A. Kufuor: President of the Republic of Ghana January 7th, 2001 – January 7th, 2009

Understand that, by your tradition and culture, you have not been central in intellectual issues and in societal development beyond the use of arms, strength, learning and errands. Unfortunately, certain traditions and sections of policy makers to the present day have carried this mindset.

Even now, with the enormous changes in your dispositions, your intellectual value to shape policy and participate in mainstream programmes towards national development is not fully appreciated by sections of policy makers and political/ traditional rulers. The reason for this situation could be partly cultural and partly lack of consistent show of maturity on issues of concern by you. It could also be deliberate.

A lot of changes are taking place on the continent. With the changing environment came different needs and aspirations. As the society grew and changed in the process, our thinking,

80

outlook and orientation did not adapt fast enough. We should have changed with it. First, in our mental disposition; and second, the hard step of taking practical actions towards that new mental orientation; a situation where the youth would be seen as an integral part of the society not only on youth related issues but on other national challenges as well. This is not to ignore the reality that, cultural webs are preventing the youth from breaking free to grow early.

There is always the issue of 'lack of capacity' on your part. Even though there may not be much argument about this point, there is a point those making the capacity argument are missing. That is, the maturation period for you has shortened. Whereas life began at forty (40) for some generations, you are compelled to take up equal life challenges at age twenty-five (25). For some of you, life begins as early as seventeen (17). Today, you are more expressive, knowledgeable and have so much available for you to learn and acquire enough within a relative short span of time.

You are capable of handling many challenges. Many of you are bred, prepared and ready. This point notwithstanding though, it is important to observe that the capacity of the youth in such issues as development and frontal roles in nation building would require long term grooming. This cannot be achieved by getting a certificate or sitting on the sidelines. It is by participating in the development process that you could learn and acquire skills needed to be meaningfully active in the society.

By the time the mantle of responsibility is to be passed or acquired, you should be ready and must have acquired the capacity required to qualify you to be an active player in the affairs of your society. The fact of life is that, 'no one would give it to you on a silver platter'. 'It (change) is never easy'. You would have to work for it...you would have to earn it'.

We can really be assured by hope that, in an open and free thinking society, there would be a tomorrow where the society would permit you to put your skills to use for the common good and benefit. A tomorrow where political parties and governments would follow consistent programmes of industrialisation, entrepreneurship and skills education to create the much talked about fertile environment for your development.

The Role Of The Society

Furthermore, the society should also be committed to industry friendly policies in low taxes and in free zones, incentives such as tax rebates, long term low interest loan facilities for small businesses, regular supply of utility, low energy cost and other relativities.

We need a society where politicians would be committed to the implementation of programmes rather than endless talk-shops of policy sessions.

In such a society, basic facilities like toilets, urinals, hospitals, basic schools and electricity would no longer be a privilege. Additionally, the society should ensure that, the minimum skill, an ability to read and write, should be enough platform for you to earn a decent living.

In the hope of this tomorrow's society, demand from politicians that as the culture changes, they would make the resulting society better for everyone as much as no one sees it as a luxury or an aberration today; for a pepper seller to use a mobile phone to transfer money to her suppliers in the village.

There is a hint of thought that, this society was created out of natural consequences and that, there is no conscious design to deny you an industrial or technological base. Even though this position could be given the benefit of doubt, do not accept this notion. The question begging to be answered is that, how do we manage to fail when others succeed? Many countries have all done it for their youth. Why can't we do it?

An Effective Youth Policy Is Your Right

A rigorous attempt to implement Youth policy is not a favour but a right and government should consider it as important as any other policy programme. The youth policy should seek to address challenges and furthermore, usher you into the twenty-first century, even though we are many years into it. It must be ICT oriented, reward hard work, punish crime, avoid discrimination, and inspire the generation. At the core, it should be a policy for the nation and not public relation document for any political tradition or culture.

Do not leave the task of your development to political leadership alone, but being mindful of how power lines run sometimes into suspicious quarters and the 'excellent and truthful' commitment of politicians. It should be said that, demand that business leaders, industrialists, the churches, non-governmental organisations, and entrepreneurs should be given a voice in the consideration and implementation of any such document under the management of a National Youth Authority. Demand and advocate for accountability.

Food For Thought

Events of a time evidently tend to have influence on the activities of those of that period. As a continent, we have gone through turbulent political and, more so, social periods. Our founding fathers and the generations which came after lived through such periods. Within the limitations of that time, they acted and created a society, either by design or accident, befitting them.

Your current generation may chastise them for building a weak society, as much as tomorrow, later generations would, with the benefit of hindsight, criticise you for many things. As such, you must tread cautiously in humility and purposefulness as you strive to advocate for your dream society so that you do not step on toes and make enemies who would turn to haunt you later in the day.

The truth of history is that, you should not be guided only by the successes of earlier generations but their failures as well. Their failures make you wiser as much as they may anger and irritate you.

Few of you believe in this society. It is a general consensus that there is so much dislocation in the society, yet it is difficult 'to set the world straight'. The old ways still holds on to the reigns of authority and power, which sowed and still nourishes the status quo.

They have a stake in the society; indeed, a greater stake and hold every right to defend what they have built or were entrusted with by earlier generations. What you ought to ask for, more persistently of course, is an opportunity to help shape the society to reflect current times and their needs.

Time May Influence Dreams

Time has ushered you into a paradigm where information is cheaper, faster, more shared and knowledge abound. Breakthroughs in science and technology now border on miracles. Some even go to space as tourists. Heart transplant is now a common place procedure.

You have the best opportunity to make impact on the society than any other generation before you. Times have changed and you need to take advantage of it.

Knowledge is no longer the preserve of the few whose parents and family names command fear and respect. These realities have affected the society.

It is not a requirement of development for your current generation to go through the rough and tumble earlier generations went through. Not long ago, in Ghana, it took seventeen (17) years to prepare for University education under the old educational system. Today, it is only twelve (12). The era of log books and slide rules have long past not because they gave wrong figures; rather, faster and efficient ways of accounting and mathematical computation have been invented and mathematics and accounting practice have gone steps further.

It is no secret that leadership: political, business, traditional and religious, are not unaware of the challenges in the society in providing opportunities for you and the conventional wisdom surrounding the miracle of time. Thus, time would not wait for any society which fails to make adequate provisions for its youth in acquiring the knowledge and competences needed to be useful and competitive. And so, it is important to make sure politicians get this message.

Your Generation Needs Different Tools

Time brings in its wake new opportunities, benefits and challenges. Worth noting is the fact that, tools required for accessing the opportunities in the current times are quite different from those used in generations long ago. Likewise, the tools employed to meet the challenges of today generations would be different from those required for the future.

Thus, it should be acknowledged that the tools of survival of one generation might be obsolete in relation to new and emerging challenges. Neither could these tools be useful to a later generation nor offer much support to their original generation in the context of current times. As such, it is important to point out to the society to employ tools which are effective, reliable and lasting in the face of current challenges and opportunities. Furthermore, it is necessary for you to continually learn and acquire new knowledge. This endeavour would make you all the more useful and an integral resource to the society as you conveniently become agents of new learning and emerging knowledge.

A Time Comes When A Leader Should Quit

The limitations of human strength, weakness and desire, make it more important for older generations at a point in time to give way to a new and energetic generation to carry on.

No single generation can fight forever nor deliver the promise. There comes a time when desire gives way and you are no longer challenged to do anything but to consolidate what you have achieved, even though outmoded and obsolete. This is the time to bow out and take full credit for your work. If you stay, you make the society stagnant, unproductive and uncompetitive. You would kill the spirit of the society. The eventual consequence could be chaotic as new forces fight for position and a voice in the affairs at hand.

Beyond the sanguine observation above lies a reality. Considering the degree of wealth scramble, materialism and degeneration of values, the biases and lack of serious efforts on the part of leadership and statecraft, one finds it difficult to say that the old ways would give in easily to the new. The new has to work for the baton. The society is not poised any time soon to deliver the needed opportunities.

Some Leaders Could Be A Threat To Your Development

The self-indulgence and excesses of the centres of power and or around it are disquieting. Very few care, and paying lip service has become the order of the day. Not a week passes without a statement from a politician, religious monarchs, traditional authorities, business leaders and interest groups urging support for the youth or crying over the youth wasting their lives on crime or offering suggestions no policy maker would heed or commit political capital to.

Leaders of society (politicians, religious monarchs, traditional authorities, business leaders and interest groups) for some time now have been accused of immoral acts, unethical behaviours and 'abominations' in our society. Political leaders churn out lies, scheme and swindle without the slightest reservation. The clergy, the backbone of our contemporary moral code, have over the years been involved in many unmentionable sinful acts you can think of including adultery, rape, extortion, sorcery, and visa racketeering.

Traditional leaders, long held as the custodian of our traditional value systems, flout the very values they are supposed to guard without missing a heartbeat. Stool lands are sold to multiple buyers and resources accrued from the sales are used for personal gains. Business leaders evade taxes, cheat consumers and sell all sort of products without recourse to public health and safety, while regulators accept bribes to put consumers at peril.

Abused Young Ladies

In a society of scarce opportunities, many a young lady do not secure jobs or maintain the same without having to sacrifice their pride and dignity. Some of you have merely been turned into some sort of prostitutes, pushed by circumstances and deception to deny yourselves your dreams and sense of purpose and dignity. Many of you roam from one place to another, attending supposed interviews at odd hours.

Eventually, the promised jobs never come and by coercion, weakness and the ploy of sweet tongue and mixture of fear, some of you are turned into 'house servers', serving the appetite of the nation wreckers at end-of-year parties, weekend orgies, escorts and special occasions.

What A Society: Your Talent Could Be Your Curse

Young brilliant men have lost their jobs because at the wrong time, they talked. Most importantly, because at the wrong time they showed they had talent, wisdom, boldness and commitment to back their drive and motivation. Their talent which is supposed to be their blessing has turned out to be their curse.

A Big Shame!

There is no need for reassurances anymore. Neither is it necessary to pacify the gods of the land nor cry out to them for mercy or help. The land is weak from hopelessness. The institutions of our society painstakingly established by those long gone are crumbling. Department of Social Welfare, the Police Service, Chieftaincy and the Clergy are all failing to measure up to the requirements of the times. This is not as a result of external forces, The West, or the usual standard excuses.

It is simply because of the failure of leadership, of policy and negligence. Many leaders have forgotten the values which established our societies in the first place.

Politics may have failed you. Many of your leadership entrusted with statecraft have only ended up destroying institutions so that there would be no challenge to their plunder. As long as the mindset, mentality and drive of a large section of leaders dwell on plundering, you should have an innate fear for the future.

As a precaution, the call is in no way saying that all the leaders of your society are irresponsible or 'wicked' as are being echoed in certain circles; but that, many of those who have held the reigns of political, economic, social and cultural powers have not been there for the society and a large section of you.

The society you live in is their creation and if, indeed, what you see is a great society, then let it be said they did well like Nkrumah, Gandhi, and Mandela, or any of our great heroes. On the other hand, if indeed the society you live in today is as poorly equipped as it is being portrayed here, with neither hope nor adequate opportunities for you to live a dignified life, then you should not hesitate to say, they have failed the society.

The fact is that, there is not much to cherish about this society. Many of you flock to foreign lands, with some few exceptions though, to live in questionable conditions without dignity or respect. Such conditions should urge you to admit the true state of our society and make a genuine protest to politicians, traditional and business leaders for reforms. These leaders need to botton up and make the decision to make a conscious effort to have a change of mind.

Furthermore, they need to put in place programmes which would necessitate the building of a healthy society. We still have in us what it takes to attain our dreams.

CHAPTER 8

DIFFERENT CLASSIFICATIONS OF THE YOUTH

'The youth is the greatest gift of God to the Society'.

Mother Theresa (26th August 1910 – 5th September 1997; Born Agnes Gonxha Bojaxhiu, A Catholic Nun of Albanian Ethnicity and Indian Citizenship

There are different classes of you by virtue of your orientation, dreams, environment and place in the society. There are six categories of you identified here based upon further categorisation, your willingness to stand by your dreams, your preparedness and views of life.

The first group is those of you who by blood or association belong to the ruling class. We shall refer to you as the *pets*. There are three categories of the pets. These are those who are privileged by blood. The others are those privileged by their association with the 'kids' or close relatives of the privileged. The third category is those picked and groomed by the status quo to serve their interests. For their current or future service, they enjoy all the privileges a bloodline would. In the course of such grooming, they learn to think, act and assume the character and hobbies of their benefactors.

The second group are those of you whose body and mind tills the soil and mills the corn for the ruling class, only to make it to their mouths. We shall refer to you as the *workers*.

The third group is those of you who either by design or false choice, have thrown your lives away. You are without skills, drive, and dreams. You are the *drags*. You have resigned to passing through time without hope or purpose.

The fourth are those of you who by luck, grace or favour have found a niche and are surviving the breezes of your dreams. They do not dream big. They do not aim for the top. They aim small and for the middle level. We shall refer to you as the *babies*.

The fifth are the *eagles*. These are those of you who out of sheer work, toil, commitment and God's grace and favour have created their share of the dream. You share a belief in divine favour but strongly believe that, 'a man must earn his daily bread'. That is to say, you are prepared to work hard, sacrifice and bid your time to be mentally and psychologically prepared for your dream's journey. You would rise to the highest levels in the society.

The sixth are the mavericks.

It is worth noting that, each of you identified here, except the drags, have by training or education acquired the basic knowledge and skills required for the pursuit of your dreams.

THE CATEGORIES

The Pets

The pets by virtue of their association and networks have priorities in many endeavours. They are not dumb. They could be brilliant, hardworking and good-hearted. They could have the best that any youth could dream of. Often though, some of them are mean, lazy, easy-going, lack focus and direction and are out of touch with the rough and tumble of life in the society as it is. What is perhaps their common characteristic is that, they are unaware of the harsh realities of the world outside theirs. To them, life has just been a straight path: have a dream, go to school, get a job, startlife, live the dream and the perfect life.

Life is meaningful to them in the sense that, they have had streams of opportunities without a setback. Life is smooth, unhindered and rewarding. The irony is that, this should be the dream life of every youth. So why fault the pets for gaining from such a dream. The irritation here is that, these few youth are living at the expense of the larger youth. They live on the charity of the custodians of the society who have created this environment many of you disapprove of. They have not earned their positions. As we impress on every youth to work and acquire skills, same cannot be said of the pets. They cut through the path to achievement and fulfilment. They break the rules and operate under a cloud of privileges not available to the other youth.

This has created an imbalance in the society. Thus, the youth does not have to be the best to get what he aspires for. He does not win on merit, rather on proximity to the centre of power. He only has to be close to a power base as a gossip, sycophant or bootlicker or a pet.

The pets are not necessarily the children of the rich. Their parents or neighbourhood is connected, resourced and have within their reach what is necessary for their dreams. In our schools, workplaces and in the larger society we see them around, living the dreams of the youth. Whatever their strengths and 'goodness', they are flawed in such a way as it make them unfit for leadership roles. Their journey and proximity to abundance make it difficult for them to appreciate the harsh realities of this life so as to force them to understand the common man whom they are to represent and make decisions on their behalf. Neither are they able to sustain their worth in the absence of their godfathers and the skewed environment so created.

Leadership comes with authority, and those to be entrusted with power must themselves be in a position to appreciate the implications and consequences of their decisions.

There are many things in this life that, obviously, neither books nor story telling can bestow on you. You may read all the books and biographies of great men in life, but for one to appreciate them in a realistic manner is for one to live them. And so, it becomes a weakness of leadership, if one moves through life as the textbook would define it. This is the life of the pets. They are eloquent, boisterous and careless, unable to see beyond their noses. Their maturity is truncated by the limitlessness of opportunities available to them and spoon-feeding.

Largely, they are under the tutelage of benefactors and are unable to assert their convictions even on personal issues. For them, to live is to live for those who favoured them. When they look across their shoulders, they do so to assure themselves that, they are doing the bidding as wished.

It is worth noting that, a pet unfit for leadership today could be very qualified tomorrow by virtue of change in orientation and other experiences. This could be necessitated when the youth gains a sense of awareness and recognises his association with the environment as a means of learning and not as an accessory to exploiting the larger youth and the society or being a tool for other men's exploitative desires.

Characteristics of Pets

The pets are those you should watch out for in any struggle. They are pressured to serve as spies and informers. After all how could they pay their 'masters' back for their easy life? These are some of their characteristics:

1. They have unusually strong ties for their age within powerful circles.

2. They rise unusually fast.

3. Whereas everyone sweat through life, they float through it.

4. They have no solid principles except to do their masters' bidding and make their living.

5. They are loved and protected by the status quo. The 'big' men love them.

6. They may seem to care but if you look at them critically, it is all about pretences.

7. They are lazy, shallow and will 'buy' their way out of situations than to earn it.

Are you a pet? I urge you to refuse to be one. If you are already one, change.

The Workers

The *workers* are those anonymous labourers who are ever toiling, never resting, never having enough but live from hand to mouth. They are neither lazy nor empty. What they lack is the basic skill and orientation required by the society to make an independent living. Neither do they have what it takes to secure a rewarding future nor the orientation to appreciate the needs of the society so as to prepare themselves to meet these needs. It seems the society has no other place for them. As if they do not exist. These are the class of the youth who have tried and failed to find route to their dreams and have thus resigned to the base of the ladder.

Largely, they failed because they lacked the appropriate skills. Their hope is lost and desires for achievement no longer stir in them. They have lost the battles and have resigned to living through life as it is presented to them and to be carried by the waves of life. They are always looking for a master to serve.

This situation is not permanent though. Over time, with the experience gained from scratching the floor, purposefulness and anguish, these workers who have for a long time been at the floor could break the ceiling and make it. This is the point when their long years of hard labour and personal sufferings have woken them up and or have earned them the hard skills needed to sustain and grow in the environment independently.

The worker does not know the art of networking and is not interested in it. He is not liked and does not show interest in anyone either. His business is himself and spares no time for anyone. Intellectually, they are largely average. They are good in handicraft and technical endeavours. They quickly resign to their environment and make the most out of it.

They are survivors. They can make the most out of the little they have to keep themselves going. By this nature, they are friends of the pets; the pets courting them though, for their servitude and unquestioning attitudes.

Their state and position in the society is not only the accident of birth but also the injustice of the environment. Their strengths among others are that, they are hardworking, creative in surviving, and could make the most out of very little. It should be said that, their creativity lies in the realm of not working only in an organized environment but also in the rough and tumble all around.

Their self-interest breeds in achieving their obligations with the sole aim of survival. And even though the societies have given them little, they give so much back to it in their own right. Time could change them at any time. Furthermore, experiences and accidents could impose an attitude which would alter their character and goodwill.

The Drags

The drags are those of you who are a burden to society. They are the delinquents, drug addicts and all the youth whom society has come to clarify as 'worthless'.

The Babies

The babies are those of you who by luck, grace or favour have found a niche and are surviving the storms of life and their dreams.

As much as we tout their 'luck', it is important to note that they are also insulated from the harsh realities of the environment. The fears and darkness of the society are largely lost to them. They are lucky. They are the lucky sons of 'God' who by destiny and sheer wizardry are always right in their judgments.

These are the babies. These are the category of the youth we normally claim they have not earned their right of place, whether in industry or society. Their luck is their strength. They are lucky to be at the right place at the right time. They spot a small opening, enter it and from there work their way up. They are instantly liked and are very smart in exploiting and building little opportunities into something big. They are good at networking and attaching themselves to people. Normally they possess unique minor skills which endear them to society or people in position of influence.

Their ability to make the right choices is also one of their strengths. They are submissive, docile and obedient. Their focus is narrow, and often their energies are concentrated on their limited focus; all to one end: to ensure their physical survival. We need them to bring some level of calmness and peace to a troubled youth. In times of stress and tear and confusion, we need them as they become the cementing mix and soft voices.

The Eagles

The eagles are those upon whose shoulders the burden of leadership, responsibility and pain of failure and or success lie. They fill leadership positions in business, academia, sports, and the clergy.

They are the protectors and servants of their generations. They may not be the most brilliant or intelligent but they show the path. They are the torchbearers of generations and society. Their strength is their heart. The urge to live beyond themselves and put the interest of their generation first is one of their driving forces.

Sometimes we say, they are irresponsible to themselves because they put the welfare of others above theirs. They are the section of the youth who dares to tread where no one dares to. They break new grounds and aspire to earn their dreams through commitment, hard work, and humility. They earn their places in society. They do not believe in secondary knowledge and achievements. They identify what they want, plan for it, and pay the price required. It is not their dream to take from the society. Their ultimate drive is to give, help the weak and the poor in their reach. They avoid the cheap ways and crowd pleasing.

These youth and unique individuals are the eagles of our societies. They are strong-willed and sometimes stubborn. They appreciate what they want and are focused on it. They are creative and do not rely on the strength and toils of others to survive. By training, they have acquired the skills and knowledge necessary for the attainment of their dreams. They are selfless and, irrespective of what the society has given them, they are always willing to give more back. Indeed, they give more to their generation and society than they take from it.

They know the limit of their abilities and thus when to consult and bow to greater wisdom. They never pick on what they cannot achieve. To them, life is perpetual learning; successes and failures are part of their rise. They resolve to undertake actions, which in part contribute to their overall goal in life. These are the eagles.

The life of the eagle is neither straight nor easy. They face serious obstacles in their communal pursuit. They are usually bruised, neglected, ignored and sometimes hated. Severally and perpetually, they become the target of small minds. They are not afraid to go against the status quo, at any cost, as long as it serves a greater goal. Their goals are not the selfish goals of the greedy, little and the mean but those goals which serves the society and the poor: those who lack the basic skills to fend for themselves and have been neglected by society.

The oppositions from the environment and struggles they go through, firstly with their confidence and secondly with the realism of their dreams, strengthen and toughen them to meet the demands of their dreams.

The pursuit of dreams requires sacrifice and that, those who aspire for higher service and share of God's benevolence ought to commit more of themselves to their dreams. As the eagles chart new routes to attain their dreams, they create standards, open doors and enlighten the society that, 'there is nothing like a dead end'. These eagles are the standard bearers, door openers and pathfinders. Their paths will be the hope for the better tomorrow whilst in their challenges and trials, many find lifelong lessons and comfort.

As a society and perhaps by human nature, we do not like non-conformist. Neither do we like those who challenge the status quo. So by nature, the society is likely to challenge any system, structure, institution or personality who threatens the status quo. In extreme cases, they hunt and at all cost fight these pioneers and groundbreakers. The beauty of the struggle is that, even though the perils of the eagles grow by the hour and their troubles grow alike and friends shun them, eventually, even at the end of their strengths, they win. And with that victory, creating something better for all. Their victory is neither the triumph of money nor fame but the victory of conviction, purpose, drive, hope, and correctness over the status quo.

It should be pointed out that, this correctness does not denote that this purposeful youth is right in his pursuit. Rather, he is correct because he believed in a cause and thus the eventual victory that was won through his sufferings, blood and toil, enhances every step of the journey towards the eventual realization of his dreams and anyone on similar course.

Therefore, in our hour of need, we need people of this calibre: selfless, bold, generous and know where they are going. We need them to fasten the sinews of our society together through these rare qualities and not by the might of materialism or the meanness of little minds.

Their dreams and lonely journey tend to serve generations and societies. They are the nerve centre of their generation. They are the progressive forces manning the endeavours of statecraft. You do not become an eagle by wishing to be one. Don't wish it; you only have to live it. Do not dream it. Live it. It is only by living the life that you would come to appreciate it and sacrifice for it. For it is within this sacrifice that the essence of your dreams would lie.

The Mavericks

The mavericks are those who neither by skills, excellence, networking nor family strength are making it quickly in life. They usually have likable manners. They have subservient traits which become their source of attraction and blessings. They usually possess these traits which make them glow and shine. These could be beauty, a nice voice, oratory, even height and pleasant bodily features. To them life is about chances. Characteristically, they are jovial, easy-going, academically average and skilful in their trade. They are honest and generous. Their lives are not easy cast though. As humans, they have jolts which usually reveal them to themselves and to others. Sometimes an act of quality reveals them to us, and at other times misfortune. They are the mavericks. They can be extremely bold, reckless or lustful, going against everybody without care for careful risks. They are rare and few. They glow so fast and burn so quickly.

None of the above categories of the youth is permanent. As much as our society is dynamic in so many ways, so is each state. An experience can change *a pet* into *an eagle*. Therefore, *a worker* can acquire new orientation and take a new course in life. Irrespective of whom you see yourself to be, you need to define yourself, set your goals in life and be confident of what you want. You must further underline how you intend to achieve it. This assessment and posture is necessary to get you on the right path to your dreams.

In our environment where 'the society and government are the enemy', it is prudent to ask the fundamental questions: who am I? What do I want in life? Thus, saving yourself from being blown back and forth by the discouraging winds of the society. With little to offer, coupled with the uncertain nature of our society, it has become all the more important to answer the question, 'who am I?' before you set foot into the real world of drama and uncertainties.

If you leave this basic question to chance, you may be turned by the environment into a product the society has no need for.

CHAPTER 9

LIFE IS ABOUT PATIENCE AND TIMING

"Life is all about timing...the unreachable becomes reachable, the unavailable becomes available, the unattainable... attainable. Have the patience, wait it out. It's all about timing."

Stacy 'The Kat' Carter (Born September 1971) An American Former Professional Wrestling Valet

Life does not follow a straight path and knowledge acquired only from books does not guarantee success in life. There is, as always, a wide and infinite gap between knowledge and reality. This gap is really important to you going forward. This is critical to you in building your patience, perseverance, and learning skills, attitudes and resources necessary in making a progressive and matured growth.

The maturity here is not an issue of age but in character and maturity in understanding the ways of life and making decisions required of a wholesome human being. This critically includes making decisions which at every turn of your life would contribute to the attainment of your dreams. That is to say, gaining the maturity to overcome sensual and emotional sentiments to make decisions which would enhance the attainment of your dreams. This means the ability to overcome the strong pull of your youthful desires and senses. The senses could sometimes be blinding.

Due to the magnitude of the gap between knowledge and reality, it is important to stress the need for you to appreciate that knowing is one thing and actually having the acquired ability to execute what you know is another. For example, you may have reasonable knowledge of designing and building a dining table, but you need to appreciate that this does not mean you can get up and build a dining table. You may sketch your dream house but it does not mean you can get up and build it even if you have the capital.

Sometimes, you may shout corruption, sycophancy, greed and bad policies. Until you are faced with the reality of these flaws, it would be difficult to appreciate the enormity of how enticing these weaknesses are. The point of facing these vices in your life is your point of reality. Many who have gone through both phases of the situation attest to the cold steel of this reality: slowly tearing you apart and breaking down your defences mercilessly. If you are lucky, matured and truly principled, by grace and favour, a firm hand would hold you stable to keep you from falling. Otherwise, you would become like one of the corrupt leaders you are chastising today.

It is for this reason that you are encouraged to listen, learn and sometimes, pause to reconsider a lot of issues before making a decision or boisterously shouting at the top of your voice.

Reality is not a dream. It is your life and the lives of many who look up to you. Every step you take in the real world could lead to a worse situation, your end, or lead you to a better situation. For this reason, it is important to urge you to learn values and skills such as patience, humility, listening, purposefulness and self education.

It is important for you to acknowledge that, it is one thing being aware of a situation; another thing understanding it, another having the skills and abilities to examine it and yet another having the courage, resources and the will to make a decision to attempt to solve it. Perhaps, it is important to overcome the obstacles of the environment and solve the challenge. Yes, that is the reality largely unknown to you as a young person. It is a lot easier identifying the numerous 'evils' within our environment but a lot more complex and difficult in setting the environment right. This too is the reality.

Thus, fighting and overcoming corruption and other vices which have torn our society apart is never easy. It takes time. It is a winding course. It is never an instantaneous act. It is not a sprint race. It is more of heptathlon or a marathon. That is why it calls for patience and a listening heart and ear. It may take one man to ignite the fire for the fight against corruption and bad governance, but it would take an army and a process to achieve victory. You need an army.

It is also critical for you to accept that, short bursts of agitation cannot do, and that one of the surest ways of survival is to get to move the political leadership to take bold steps in the form of policy initiatives and effective programmes. These programmes should be backed by institutions with real mandates, timelines, resources and capacity and not personalities.

The campaign calls for patience. This could only be attained by admitting that there is so much to learn and much to prove. This is not the academic learning leading to certificate. Rather, it is the art of surviving in this world which only comes through experience, humility, cautiousness and adherence to core values such as dignity, honesty, hard work, respect for values and life.

Beware. Look and learn. Pause before you talk. Work as a group when possible.

CHAPTER 10

LIFE HAS HAPPY AND SOUR MOMENTS

"Talents are best nurtured in solitude, but character is best formed in the stormy billows of the world"

Johann Wolfgang von Goethe, German Writer, Pictorial Artist, Biologist, Theoretical Physicist and Polymath (28th August 1749–22nd March 1832)

Life has its lows and joys for everyone. Sometimes you succeed at your efforts, and at other times you face a setback. Life has a way of upsetting you. Once, a prince remarked to his senior brother, "The gods have blessed our voyage." The brother retorted, "The gods bless you in the morning and curse you in the afternoon."

Life is fraught with hurdles and roadblocks. You might do all that you have been taught and admonished to do: work hard, commit yourselves to your dreams, be patient and undertake counselling; yet, you are bound to encounter at one time or the other, one of those moments when you would question and second-guess your convictions; a time when all around you would go wrong. A period the whole world would be against you. It is a time of great confusion, stress and depression. You may lose one of the battles.

This is something you should take note of and prepare for. You may read the examination questions carefully, yet you may deviate from a question and provide the wrong answer. It is an occurrence of life. You may satisfy the requirement for a facility from your bankers, yet they may deny you the facility.

People who stumble and fall are neither toddlers nor cripples. They just missed a step and stumbled. Your test of strength and conviction lies in your rising again. When you rise, you become the more wiser, careful and stronger.

As you pursue your dreams in life, note that there are crisis periods which are devastating, crushing and cold. They are periods of uncertainty, confusion and complete darkness. They are periods when you question your own identity. They are periods when you no longer believe in yourself. They are periods of weakness and doubt. Everything seems to be against you. They are periods of loneliness.

At such periods, parents and close friends could even be against you. These are periods you come face to face with your dreams, ambitions and reality. This is the period when the beautiful world you have created in your mind is thrust into the real world. At these moments, your dreams look burnt up, you look funny, light and in blunt language, a dreamer. Fear begins to grip you. You tremble and begin to lose hope. The distressing realisation of being like everybody begins to dig in.

You are determined to be special by doing things differently; but here you are, faced with reality. You are like everyone else. There is nothing special about you. You are doing the very things everyone is doing which you are supposed to live above! "Why risk everything? Go with the masses", the silent voice of mediocrity begins to sound convincing.

At this period, you struggle within yourselves with what to believe in and even question the wisdom of your dreams. The pain of this period is sharp and deep. It may bring in its wake successive setbacks. Yet, it is only a storm. A storm you would one day look back at and smile. Stand your grounds and live above the crowd. Stand by your sacred values. Be different. Dare to be. For in your success would lie a new and hallow paths for your generation and society. You are a pioneer.

Many people hate loneliness. That is not to say to be by themselves in a room or an elevator. We are referring to the situation where no one shares your dream, vision and (or) line of thought and in such a situation find yourself heading to your destination alone. Do not be alarmed if you are alone. Your vision could be the beginning of a great thing for the nation.

Sometimes, it is like you are alone in the world. You may even be deemed insane. This period is really a trying period for every youth. If you avoid it by taking the broad path, you would become ordinary. If you persist through the narrow path, your body and mind would suffer serious stress but you would come out a better man, able to achieve great and lofty dreams in life.

Believe in your dreams

Do not give up. Do not lose hope. Focus. Pray and tap into the abundance of God. Hold on to the dreams and remember that this is just a period in your life. It would pass. The fundamental question for you to ask is: would you be a better or weaker person when this storm is over? You surely have to be a better person: disciplined, humble and hardworking.

This is the period when you make the decision to stand by what you believe in and go against everyone else or fold up. You might even be against yourself.

As a great military conqueror is reported to have once said, "You are alone when you are with the myths (your dreams)."

You may lose your grip, sense of direction and purpose. Your loneliness and state of confusion is not unique to you alone. Most people who set out to achieve their lofty dreams have found themselves at one point or the other at this stage of confusion. Ask Nelson Mandela, Kofi Annan, Mo Ibrahim and J. A. Kufuor. Ask your Father, Mother, Uncle or head of a Business.

At this moment in your life, there should be a determination and only one cry: a cry for freedom. Freedom from fear, failure and defeat; a cry for freedom from the path of failure and pain created by those before you and those long gone without leaving a good name behind. A cry to free your mind from pettiness, fear and doubt, noting that you could be another Nkrumah, Aliko Dangote, Desmond Tutu or '*The Person*' your Creator has created You to be.

For you, this moment is more critical for a number of reasons. Firstly, it defines your life. Secondly, your character is formed at this moment. Whether you would be tough, strong or a weak adult depends on what you do at this period in your life. If you persist, you become strong. If you fold and give much ground to weaknesses, cut corners, bow down to gossips and other little attitudes, that is it. You are defined and if not careful, you would remain so all your life.

How to Walk Through the Period

Even though this period is often fraught with confusion, loneliness and pain, 'you are never alone'. It is another phase in life that begets development, maturity and character formation. It is a preparatory period which you should take the opportunity to know yourself, define yourself and confirm your dreams to yourself. It is important to use this loneliness to be by yourself and assess the viability of your dreams, identify your weaknesses and chart a workable course for your future. It is a learning period.

There should be no illusions about this period. No matter how careful you are, you are likely to meet it. What matters is partly not to be ignorant about it, and partly not to wrongly assume that you are the only person going through it. Even though it is a period of fire baptism, it is a unique opportunity to test your toughness, strength and ability to stand by your beliefs and dreams in the face of reality and setbacks. Some people abandon their dreams at this stage and settle for *nothing* or *something* less. They leave their lives to 'fate'.

It is a period to come to terms with your youthful inadequacies and frailties. As a young person, sometimes untouched by life, you are boastful, naive, arrogant and careless. You have to be tested. It is Life's end of the term or semester examination. It is your final paper for your promotion. You are only promoted when you pass. It could be in marriage, business, or any of life's endeavours.

Thus, in order not to lose your path in the haze of confusion and the turbulence of this period, it is thus urged that you acquire a notebook and pen down your vision in simple itemised format as thus:

1. Write down your dreams and visions.

2. Expand them with time as your experiences open your horizon.

3. Review them through research and consultation with counsellors.

4. Claim the dreams by making them your own.

5. Be prepared to stand by them no matter the circumstances.

6. During this period, acquire the habit of noting the challenges you are facing.

7. Note any burst of inspiration and encouragement that comes to you at this period. They are plenty.

8. At the end of the storm, write down the lessons learnt.

CHAPTER 11

THE TALENT SPECTRUM

'Whatever you are by nature, keep to it; never desert your line of talent. Be what nature intended you for and you will succeed'.

Sydney Smith (1771 - 1845), English Essayist.

Beyond dreams, the euphoria, the ecstasy and joy, you would have to make time and conduct due analysis of your suitability for the dream you have so conceived for yourself. Every youth has talents and reasonably, it is appropriate to assume that dreams should bother on your talents. If you have no talent for something, dreaming of success in such a field would be a daunting task. Talent as referred to here is loosely interchangeable with skills and abilities. Without skills related to the requirements of your dreams, the dreams become only a wish which might never be achieved. In this light, it is important to note that your dreams need a foundation and a minimum amount of common sense. An ambition alone will not suffice.

It is necessary to ascertain the suitability or otherwise of your environment in its current form to meet the conditions your general dreams require. It is important to accept that the analysis of your abilities and suitability for the chosen dream, your weaknesses and deficiencies, the opportunities available to you and challenges inherent in the pursuit of your dreams are necessary in positioning yourself to achieve your dreams. The environment is never stagnant. It may improve. So it is necessary to regularly review your environment and adjust your chosen path to your dreams to reflect on it.

The Talent Spectrum would be used here to denote the analysis of one's talents in the light of his strength, weakness, opportunities and threats (SWOT).

In Model One below, the youth would be advised to make a rough list of their talents. This spectrum is tested by a basic analysis. It is within this analysis that the viability of your dream and their relativities would be clearly identified and addressed. Often, many a youth go about wearing their big dreams on their sleeves but with little effort to analyse them. We are taking this opportunity to consider your dreams in a manner expected to be free of bias and sentiments.

The SWOT, which is a basic analysis tool in business, is borrowed here due to its applicability at this instance. After all, attaining your dreams is a big business. It is represented in Model Two below.

The essential key element of the talent spectrum is your talents and how to identify them. It is important for you to carefully list the talents you think you possess. If need be, you can call a friend to help you in this endeavour. The premise being established herein is that, your talent, either innate or acquired, is critical in harnessing the skills necessary for the attainment of your dreams.

Furthermore, once your talents have been listed as preferred, you then go ahead to list the positive sides of your talents as per their contribution to your development and dreams. In other words, you are to identify how far these talents go to help in your dreams. You should be as brief and honest as possible. Honesty is critical at this point. If you exaggerate, you would arrive at conclusions which would affect your development. Remember that, it is your own life which is at the centre here.

Model One

Self Analysis Or Assessment One

Name/ Initials	Brief Description Of Yourself	**Your talents** (it is possible you would consult friends about other talents they know you to possess)	Remarks

Model Two

Self Analysis Or Assessment 2 Talent Analysis Model (TAM)

INDICATORS	LISTED ITEMS
1. Strengths Of My Talents (Talent by talent)	
2. Weaknesses Of My Talents (Talent by talent)	
3. Opportunities My Talents Present (Talent by talent)	
4. Threats To My Talents (Talent by talent)	
5. What I Ought To Do (Talent by talent)	
(CONCLUSION) General remarks worth noting down	

Model Three

Self Analysis Or Assessment 3 Dream Analysis Model (DAM)

MY DREAMS (List dreams below)	
1. or A:	
2. or B:	
3. or C:	
1. Skills and Abilities Needed To Achieve My Dreams	
2. My Personal Weaknesses To Guard Against	
3. Opportunities Dreams Offer	
4. Threats To My Dreams (From Me And External)	
5. My Remarks	

Cross Analysis

At this stage, there are some few things you know about yourself:

1. You are aware of the strengths (qualities, skills) needed to achieve your dreams.

2. You know the measure of your personal strengths.

3. You have identified threats to the dreams (from you or external). The threats from you are the bad habits and attitudes which inhibit your success. These threats include daydreaming, laziness, overt lifestyles among others.

4. You know your weaknesses with respect to your dreams.

5. You know the opportunities available to you towards the development of your talents.

At this stage, you are required to undertake another basic task.

1. It is important to list skills you lack by looking at Model Two and Model Three. It would tell you the skills you need to 'top up' *Your Talents* in order to achieve your dreams.

2. List the skills you are convinced you ought to acquire in order to achieve your dreams (you ought to consult a counsellor if you are lost as to what you need).

3. With or without the help of a counsellor, list the training or education necessary to help you achieve the skills identified in (-2-) above. But it is advisable to use the services of the school, Church or any other certified professional counsellor.

4. Make a decision as to what to do. Are you prepared to pay the price (the needed training and accompanying time and other commitments)?

5. Conclude your analysis (finalise the decision and move on. If you decided to go ahead, move on. If you said no, that is it. Pause and come back to it later.)

It is advisable here to be honest with yourself. If you fake out or you are dishonest about a talent, you are likely to arrive at false conclusions which would affect your understanding of your talents.

CHAPTER 12

THE CAREER SPECTRUM

*'Your outlook upon life, your estimate of yourself,
your estimate of your value are largely coloured
by your environment. Your whole career will be
modified, shaped, moulded by your surroundings,
by the character of the people with whom you come
in contact every day...'*

Orison Swett Marden (1850 - 1924) An American writer associated with
the New Thought Movement

This chapter largely seeks to draw a link between talents and career. There is no doubt that many of you have careers you aspire. You yearn for them, dream of them but pursue them less. This chapter is the point of 'no-more-dreams'. It is the point of reality where you set out to define yourself based upon those parts of your dreams which are realistic and achievable. It is the first step on the ladder to your dreams. Those dreams your abilities could help you to achieve. It is not worth dreaming forever or pursuing dream careers you are neither suited nor prepared for.

The *Career Spectrum* denotes that, the combination of your skills, drive, preparedness and opportunities should determine your career choice. It should not be about ego, blind dreams, ambitions and or mad drive to catch up with a friend, your parents' wish and 'community' quest for you. The reasoning is that, you would develop faster and climb higher in a field your talents can match up to. A trained psychologist would do better as a career counsellor than as a software developer.

If a psychologist has ambitions to be a software developer, the best option for him is to retrain in computer programming or a related field. Otherwise, his career should be in counselling or psychology related fields.

At this point, a table is provided below to help you get an idea of the relationship between your talents and dreams. It is worth remembering that nothing should be left to chance in assessing yourself for the dreams you have.

As much as possible, take pains to consider the smaller issues you would normally ignore. The bigger issues, of course, are also important. The smaller issues serve as the gel which cements the bigger issues of your dreams together.

Requirement	Values	Scoreboard	Remarks
Talents/Skills/ education	HND accounting, two years working experience, certificate in Sage 500 accounting software etc...	55%	
Drive			
Preparedness			
Confidence			
Opportunities/ Environment			
Satisfaction			
Nominal Average Score			

For clarity, it is important to explain certain aspects of the table above. *Requirement* denote the basic key variables and or attributes you would need to consider in determining to pursue your dreams. You might not have all of them in adequate measure, but whatever the level of your present skills, the fact still remains that they are essential requirements in your considerations.

These requirements should be in equal measure for you to create balance within yourself and the environment. This balance is important in ensuring that you are not carried away by sentiments and unwarranted dreams.

The argument is not to the effect that you would be in a situation to scientifically establish an equal measure of the requirements. What is being encouraged here is to make a careful note of the various issues at stake and act in a calculated manner to position yourself as you set off on your career.

The *values* denote the list of qualities, issues and or skills which in your opinion or in the opinion of counsellors or career consultants corresponds to the items in the *requirement* column. This column should be the exact skills, networks and resources which in the estimation of your counsellors are needed. There is the need for honesty here. This is because your later conclusions would be based on these values you have identified. Insincerity on your part could lead to biased conclusions which would mislead you to either undervalue or overestimate your preparedness for the career dreams. You are free to add a value or another as your dreams would require or prepare a new table altogether.

On the *scoreboard*, you are casually required to assign a nominal figure to correspond to the values listed earlier. There is no immediate need for any standard deviations, correlations or any calculus here. Casually score yourself as you consider yourself fit for the career. If you are unsure of the values you need for your specific career, consult friends or a career advisor. Take the exercise in this column as one of the easy puzzles you solve while killing an afternoon away.

In the remarks column, make a point or two as to issues which are outside the box but relative to your dreams and talents. Sometimes, there are critical issues you may want to come back to later.

In the end, find the average of your scores.

In scoring, avoid high end values such as 90% - 100%. Environmental factors, maturity and reality make it unnecessary to be 90% qualified.

Finally, on your chart, find the simple average of your scores. Forty percent (40%) is the border line. If you fall below it, you would have to reconsider putting your pursuit on hold until you have improved your requirements (Skills).

When you finally score your magic number of 41% and decide on the path you wish to take, say to yourself, 'I Am For It' and set out to look for the 'job' that would set you on the journey to that career. It is your skills and their development and not dreams and ambitions which would determine the degree of success of achieving your dreams. Remember, whatever your score, it is only the starting mark. There is so much yet to learn.

As has been noticed and analysed above, talents and skills become the obvious bedrock for your dreams and career springboard. Talents ought to be developed, nurtured and guarded in order for you to achieve your dreams. Your talents, potentials, skills, environment and opportunities sell you to employers. In the case of self-employment, it helps you to manage your firms and endeavours effectively and efficiently.

Drive is critical to the pursuit of your dreams. You should be motivated to commit resources and energy to the pursuit of your dreams. Motivation energises you. It gives you hope to go on when all else fails you. Drive is an inner force which keeps you going irrespective of physical constraints. It helps you to manoeuvre emotional constraints as well. At certain times, it impels you to focus and commit to your dreams. Without drive, you lose much of your edge, energy and motivation.

If you are not prepared for a dream career, it is difficult to give out your best to please your employer or achieve the business or career goals you have set for yourself.

By preparedness, the reference is in the situation where you are equipped with the skills, resources and abilities needed for the set goals. Additionally, it should be added that, mental preparedness is reflected by right attitude, conviction, possession of core values, toughness, perseverance, readiness, enthusiasm and the desire to learn and grow.

BOOK TWO

DREAMS

'The size of your dreams must always exceed your current capacity to achieve them. If your dreams do not scare you, they are not big enough.'

Ellen Johnson Sirleaf (Born 29th October1938)

Her Excellency is the 24th President of Liberia.

'The dreamers are the saviours of the world. He who cherishes a beautiful vision, a lofty ideal in his heart, will one day realize it. Cherish your visions. Cherish your ideals. To desire is to obtain; to aspire is to achieve. Dream lofty dreams, and as you dream, so shall you become. Your Vision is the promise of what you shall one day be. Your Ideal is the prophecy of what you shall at last unveil. The greatest achievement was at first and for a time a dream'.

James Allen

'The best way to make your dreams come true, is to wake up'

Paul Kagame (Born 23rd October, 1957)

His Excellency is the 6th and current President of Rwanda

121

CHAPTER 13

DREAMS

'We grow great by dreams. All big men are dreamers. Some of us let these great dreams die, but others nourish and protect them; nurse them through bad days till they bring them to the sunshine and light which comes always to those who sincerely hope that their dreams will come true'.

Woodrow Wilson, December 28th, 1856 - February 3rd, 1924; 28th President of the United States of America

Dreams are sometimes like mirages. They turn beggars into kings, slaves into masters and the homeless into estate owners overnight. In the dream world, everything is great. There are neither tears nor sorrows. It is a world of perpetual bliss. A world of abundance, where there is neither scarcity nor disappointment. All is well. Peace and Happiness reign. Within this bliss, you have hope, purpose and light to guide you as you pertain to the ideals of your lofty dreams.

These dreams drive you in your endeavours. They may be bold or moderate but remember, the bold dreams are the ones which leave your footprints in history. Thus, 'the glory and memories of men belong to those who follow their bold visions'. Or as it is said, 'fortune favours the bold'. No dream is too big to be achieved. As long as your mind can conceive it, it can be achieved.

122

It is worth reiterating that in the context of personal development, dreams are a source of motivation. They are useful in serving as guidelines in your psychological compass as you navigate through the harsh realities of life. It is always shouted that, you should 'dream big'. BIG is good. In the context of fostering motivation, it is useful to you.

You need to dream of a society better for all and work to achieve it. Work to build a society better for the Libyan youth, Rwandan youth, South African, Congolese and the Tanzanian. A society not controlled by a few, whether directly or by proxy; but controlled by all and for the good of all. A country where the standard of wealth is neither measured by financial status nor by temporal power, but by highest moral values, vision, and purposefulness which have once created and sustained great empires and nations.

Without doubt, most of you wish to live a modest life: a decent house, a wife, a husband, a family and a car or alternative means. You aspire to live a dignified life in your country. It is the dream of many of you to be part of the society, wishing for the opportunity to develop yourself and to contribute to the national efforts. This is a basic dream with sound elements of contentment and realism.

Therefore, as you dream and struggle on great visions, certain elements and values such as boldness, courage, single-mindedness, perseverance, endurance, firmness and steady-mindedness should be part of your attitude and character. Thus, dreams alone do not survive in the real world. Without the right attitudes and balance, they would not grow beyond your nose and ego.

Dreams and Reality

Dreams and reality are not friends but always go hand in hand. Sometimes you get more than you dreamt for and at other times you get less. Why this is so is a complex mix of issues unrelated to the course and lure of this work. The thrust here is that, there should be an understanding that there is a big difference between dreams and reality as stated in an earlier chapter. Thus, dreams should largely be a guide. Dreams should be the inspirational road map of your life's ambition; a motivator and a silent voice in the storms of life; a friend adding purpose and energy to your life.

A dream goes against reality. It neither despairs nor accepts the failures of life. It is a platform for miracles and impossibilities; a friend who drives away fear, despair, failure and always positions you in the right light for you to receive success and fulfilment at the right times. Ultimately, dreams are just dreams unless they are horned by reality; but unfortunately, the reality as determined by the society is not controlled by you. So many dreams wander and fade away.

You must have dreams; dreams which would uplift you to the level of your aspirations so that you can contribute meaningfully to your personal development, that of your family and the society. Your dreams should challenge you to develop with a sense of purpose in life. Dream to be one of the few people who dare to break new grounds. Those rare citizens who set the pace for their generations and posterity and upon whose visions the burden of their generation and the future lies. These are the eagles. This is the big dream.

Short Term, Medium and Long Term Dreams

For the purpose of clarity, let us consider dreams in terms of short-term, medium-term and lifetime. Short-term dreams are usually expected in less than a year or two. They could be synonymous with New Year's resolutions, semester grade goals or a month's resolution. The short-term dream should feed the medium-term dreams. In other words, short term goals serve as the foundation for medium-term dreams and lifelong goals.

Medium-term dreams are relatively between three to five years. They could be courtship leading to marriage and timelines for young professionals. They could also be business start-up goals. Or career progression goals.

The lifelong dreams are long term and stay with you until death. It is the ultimate dream that would be the essence of your life. What you would be remembered for. They could be personal or communal.

It is worth noting that, short-term goals should feed medium-term dreams and thus the long-term dreams. They should neither be disjointed nor non-aligned. Short-term dreams should help you to achieve your medium-term dreams by providing you with the skills and opportunities needed for the medium-term dreams. On the other hand, medium-term dreams should provide you with the skills, competences, opportunities and attitudes necessary for achieving your long-term dreams. The path from the short term through the medium to the lifelong dreams should be seamless. Each preceding stage should provide a platform for the next.

The Successful Youth

It is your right to dream to be successful in life. This success should not be solely determined by either material wealth or personal gain, but by how much you would give back to society. This is the greatest sacrificial story of all. And if you should dream to be the one 'who gave all to the society', then you would truly be a successful person in the life of the society. You do not have to be a politician or a 'huge' figure to give back to society. I wonder how many of these figures have given much back to society. Your little would be enough for someone in the society.

Sincerely, you have to be yourself. Be who you are and give back what you can; and truly, you would be remembered for what you were able to afford to give to society. Mother Theresa, Wangari Maathai, and Esther Ocloo lived a life of service. We cannot say they were rich in the material sense. But there is no doubt that, their names would live on for their services to humanity.

The Pursuit Of Dreams Is A Lonely Journey

The pursuit of dreams is a lonely journey you are being urged to make. It is an extremely lonely journey, especially in your environment, considering what it has turned many of you into. It is a journey with few friends. There would be frustrations, betrayals and a feeling of getting late in life. You would hear voices such as; 'you are behind'; 'you are naïve'. Do not be deterred. Your eyes are in your head. You are building a future that would have a place in the hearts and minds of your peers and generations; a future which would put your mind at peace and give you fulfilment in your old age and beyond.

Be assured that when your groundbreaking dreams come to light, those who despised and avoided your company in the days of tears and toil would come back to you. Whatever you lost would be paid back by your achievements. It is a simple truth. If you choose to go with the multitude on the common and easy path, you are likely to be as common as the path you have taken. There is no shame about this. It is a choice you have made and it should be respected as such. There are many people like you, taking few or no risks at all in life and truly no one remembers their names. They would always say –'I knew you'; 'I knew Kofi Annan'. 'I even bought food for him and paid his rents'.

Three Dimensions Of Dreams

It has been said that 'dream should be attainable'. Indeed they should be. You should have the potential, will, strength and motivation to achieve your dreams and, above all, be willing to sacrifice for them. You may not have the means to achieve your dreams at first thought. What is necessary to note is that, dreams have limits. They can set the upper and lower levels of your life. As has been noted, dreams are just dreams. They motivate and remind you of what you wish to achieve in life.

There is a side of dreams which may send you into a spiral of ecstasy so much to the extent that, it takes all your time, energies and steals any sense of reality from you. This type of dream is dangerous and shutters any chance of you achieving anything. If not prompted, it destroys and turns you into a lazy wisher. This type of dream is called daydreaming.

Dreams have three broad dimensions. These are what you aspire to achieve, which is the dream; how you achieve the dreams, which is the path; and what you indeed achieve, which is the fulfilment. It should be added that, dreams should be clear, achievable and specific. Time is not a basic consideration here. This life is not a race. Some get rich at twenty, others at twenty-seven and still others at forty and even at fifty.

Once you are set on your dreams, then comes the question of how to achieve them. There are as numerous paths to achieving your dreams as there are individuals. The stories you hear about achievers should not be your templates, because the environments could be different; the timing, societal pull, family support and other relativities could be different. Even your skills level, motivations, preparedness and drive could all be different. You need to set out on your own considering yourself in the light of who you are. The stories of achievers should only tell you that you can also make it.

Steps Towards your Dreams

At this stage, it is well assumed that you have already shot for your dreams in your heart. Or for simplicity purposes, might have written them down in your journal or diary. The next proposed step is to make time to undertake some simple exercises as thus: (recapping the Dream Spectrum in a different light)

1. Write your dreams again on paper.

2. Ask yourself or find out what it would take to achieve your dreams.

3. Ask yourself: what skills do I need in order to achieve my dreams?

4. What other resources do I need?

5. How do I acquire the skills and resources required to achieve my dreams?

6. Identify factors which would militate against you.

7. Find out: how do I avoid or overcome these mitigating factors?

8. Pause with an open mind and reflect on the questions and statements above.

It is worth noting that going through these eight (8) steps could take a year, two or even three. The waiting would be worth it if you are indeed to succeed. This is your future and life under consideration, so be patient and pay attention to details.

What to do after question number eight (8).

a. Remember to write down the answers to these questions

b. Read over them a couple of times.

c. Note which ones require action. Prioritise the actions in order of magnitude (you may consult a friend or counsellor).

d. Group the actions into timelines (one (1)–six (6)-month, one-year and three-year periods)

9. Keep these solutions in mind.

10. Revisit your dreams as in question 1.

11. Ask yourself: what is the first step?

12. Take the first step.

13. Remind yourself of question 3.

14. Then work hard towards achieving the dreams.

These basic steps should be used as a guide rather than a rule.

CHAPTER 14

DREAMS AND CAREER ROUTES MODEL

"Young citizens are influential agents of change and innovation when they find a space where they can voice their views, develop leadership capacity and interact creatively,"

Sanjay Pradhan, Vice President, World Bank Institute (WBI)

Attaining one's dreams go beyond poetry, colourful language and excitement. It rests on sound wisdom and pragmatism. It includes a lot of guidance. Despite the fact that it is your sole responsibility to make decisions about your vision and future, their realisation might not rely on your strength alone. There are people who have travelled on that path before you. It is advised you consult them. Sometimes you read from their autobiographies and listen to stories told of them by those who knew them. Sometimes you learn from associations. At other times, you learn from the streets. The wisdom herein is that, to achieve your dreams, you need other people's collective knowledge, experiences, wisdom and resources.

In the spirit of this insight, it is worth noting that every person you meet is important in your cumulative collection of wisdom, skills and attitudes towards the attainment of adequate strength for your dreams and vision. Every word you hear could warn, teach, inspire, correct or discourage you on your journey. Thus, you are alone when dreaming but never alone when you set out to achieve the dreams.

In this light, a dream model is designed to help you chart an upward course. The dream diagram has seven (7) stages, all of which are of equal importance. Your basic skills usher you from the dreamland to the growth platform. Between the dreamland and the growth platform is the progression stage. From the growth platform, you begin the tedious and painful journey to the achievement platform.

Career Route Model

The Dreamland

The dreamland is the stage at which most of you dream to be kings, queens, great achievers, presidents, poets, inventors and great men and women.

This stage is in three (3) sections: the level of pure dreams, the level of awareness and level of complete awareness.

The Level Of Pure Dreams

This is the level which bothers on 'madness'. It is the stage where you wish for anything and everything. The stage when you dream of becoming God, Jesus, the marrying, the most beautiful woman in the world or the richest man in the world. And with this, you would change the world and make it better for all. No more wars. No sorrows and no pain. A world of perpetual bliss. You have no sense of reality, nor awareness of your environment. It is a stage of pure fantasy. It is the stage when in your days of maturity you would look back and say, 'I was really mad.'

This is the stage at which you would roam from Paris to Abuja to Accra. You would find yourself at lunch with the President. Better still, on a hot date with your dream woman, only to wake up and find yourself in a crowded market with the sun beating down your back or hungry in a queue buying food from a bush-canteen. At this level, there are serious emotional fluctuations, bursts of anger, depression and loneliness. Everything is out of reality. It is all a mirage. You even see yourself in a mirror as the Sultan of Brunei with servants attending to you.

Since dreams are what they are, all dreams are possible. The difference here is that, you are asking for something that you are neither suited nor ready for. You cannot be God under any circumstance besides your fantasies. Neither are you Aliko Dangote. You are YOU.

This level is bound by time, yet you may be oblivious of it. You may wish to date Minnie Dlamini, which may be realistic in say ten (10) years but the question is, would she be at her peak in ten years for you to hold on to the dream of dating her? Or would she be available? She may be married. Time brings growth, maturity and transformations.

The Level Of Awareness

The second stage is the level of awareness. This is the stage where you come to know that, you cannot be God, Jesus or Mohamed. At this stage, you come to another realisation that you cannot wish your way through life.

There is normally some level of confusion at this stage. Sometimes you are aware that, you are wishful and yet you find it difficult to identify what you need to do to make it a reality. You would clearly see through the 'madness' of your dreams, yet there is no way for you to tell yourself to abandon them. The dreams are too appealing.

This stage is clearly frustrating. Even as you identify the fruitlessness of your dreams, you find it almost impossible to discard the dreams as unattainable. The lure of these dreams is enticing. The dreams have the attractiveness to hold you even as you see them as fantasies.

Level Of Complete Awareness

This is the stage leading to the reorganisation of your dreams. At this stage you are fundamentally aware of the madness and limitation of your dreams. You are aware of your environment and the fruitlessness of pure dreams. Through a painful clash of emotions, reality and criticism, you have become fully aware that your dreams need something more.

During this period, you have acquired the courage to make an attempt to discard those 'God-dreams'. You have learned to reorganise the dreams in a basic, logical and achievable manner. At this level, you begin to refine your dreams to reflect reality. You are aware of your environment, its effects on your dreams and you are willing to take the necessary painful initiatives to align them to reality. You have overcome your sentimentalities.

One key development at this level is that, you become intrinsically aware of the need to physically develop by acquiring certain skills.

The Rise Gap

The rise gap is very critical to the dream quest. This is the stage of using your knowledge bank. You begin the quest by rightly employing your knowledge through formal and informal means to enhance your journey. This is where you learn of the environment in real terms.

Furthermore, you begin to acquire basic emotional, mental and physical finesse prerequisite to attaining your dreams. You should be able to identify opportunities and use these opportunities to further your development aims.

What is being said is that, at this stage you have acquired the basic skill needed to move from one stage to the other on your journey towards the achievement of your dreams. You have grown with time through experience. As you gain knowledge, you review your dreams and align them to reality. The knowledge and skills base you have acquired at this stage is not the complete sense of what is needed.

Rather, it is the basic aptitudes needed for the initial journey. It is the stage you begin to go beyond the minimum knowledge base to make them useful to yourself and society. In simple terms, it is the stage you receive the 'fifty-percent (50%)' pass mark in skills, aptitude and common sense but must decide to move to the next nevel or continue to be a perpetual dreamer.

The Growth Platform

The growth platform is the stage where you take up a job. It could either be private or public sector or self-employed. It is the take-off stage. You continue to expand your skill and knowledge base through practical means, having acquired the basic skills needed to start the pursuit of your dreams. That is to say, academic knowledge base or technical skills acquired through artisanship, apprenticeship, and informal trade. The other form of skills acquisition is skills by traditional education and lifelong education. It could be in any discipline: arts, engineering, banking, investment, entrepreneurship and other related issues.

During this level, you prepare to chart the cause for your dreams. You may seek to obtain the dreams through the formal structure or at a point use the acquired knowledge to branch out and seek fulfilment in private ownership. The knowledge, awareness and skills gained at this level is merely basic and could be used to push you to a certain level but would not be enough for you to achieve your eventual dreams.

It is also important for you to come to terms with the fact that, there are levels of frustrations at this stage. They are more pronounced in the case of the more adventurous and ambitious. You would find comfort at the thought of having come this far and settled on a profession or career. You are faced with an enormous opportunity ahead of you but at the same time, you are hindered by the reality that you cannot grow overnight. It is like standing on top of a mountain, you could see the dream afar but to reach it, it would take some amount of time to descend into the valley and climb severally and painfully again in order to reach the destination. You are walking in the valley of growth.

Be reminded that, you are continually required to learn and employ the knowledge to develop yourself in order to move to the next level. Most importantly, be aware that there are many experiences you are yet to acquire. Learning and patience are key success factors at this level. This stage is the starting block. The stage where every conceivable preparation has been made to enable you move towards your vision. You have no illusions about what you want at this point.

Another distinctive factor of this stage is that, even though you have settled on your dreams, there is little knowledge as to, firstly, how to achieve them and, secondly, control over institutions, culture and the environment controlling the journey towards the achievement. This aspect is something lost to you. It is very latent but powerful to the extent that, it can hold back the realisation of the vision for the rest of your life. As such, it is important to learn the ropes and align your chosen path with reality regularly.

It should be added that, there is no timeline to this period. You interact with the environment till you find a niche and follow to your dreams. The bursts of frustration, depressions, high spirits, and pain you go through at this stage are less painful as a result of your understanding of the environment in part and secondly, because of your ability to control these bursts and see them as obvious part of the growing process.

The more you acquaint yourself to contain these periods, the better you would be placed to ensure that you grow strongly and more prepared for the journey you intend to embark upon for the sake of your dreams. Furthermore, you should be prepared to sacrifice time, energy, resources and sometimes even comfort to achieve your dreams.

Indeed such sacrifices are welcomed and required because you believe in the dream and you are prepared to see that they are achieved. You have learnt to survive through the dream at this stage. You have a glimpse of the future, the dream, but lack the total capacities to pursue them.

The Progression Stage

The progression stage is perhaps the most crucial and most hazardous. This is the stage when you begin the actual ascent towards your dreams. The youth now has a foot on what they believe would take them up or as in the case of the self-employed, they have that job which would take them towards the dreams and that spark which would set them up to achieving their dreams.

This is the actual process of working to achieve your dreams. You start the painful task of growth, motivated by the hope of a better future. It could take a lifetime or may not be realised at all. This stage is the most perilous. Personal weaknesses, lack of confidence, human interferences and discouragement are key elements of the setbacks you are likely to encounter.

One of the key elements in succeeding through the progression period is discipline. Knowing what you want and planning for it, is not enough. You need to be focused, direct, frank and be able to deny yourself certain youthful pleasures. This includes controlling your passions and exercising your energies to achieving the dream.

Certain values are important here as well. That is, it is important for you to comply with certain basic attitudes such as time and self-management, effective communication, networking, honesty, trustworthiness, humility, team work and goodwill. These are some of the essential values which the youth needs in order to survive the turbulent world, and upon such, build on the needed capacity to achieve their dreams.

The paths to most dreams are never straight. They are never achieved in one leap. Neither are they achieved by a continuous upward progressive manner nor upon the magic of one silver bullet. As someone said, 'you reach and you fall'. Sometimes you may go up and at other times you fall. You may be so close to it and yet you would fail to achieve. When you encounter such a time, remember that you are never the first and would never be the last. It is one aspect of the journey. It is a winding path, but you would get there not on your own terms and time alone.

Furthermore, it is important for you to remember that you would need other unforeseen resources to achieve your dream. It is for this reason, among others, that it is important to build effective human relations with achievers. Thus, people who have gone past your stage in life successfully. These are people who have made it in life. Largely, at this stage, every decision you make should contribute to attaining your dreams.

Five Routes To Achieving Your Dreams

Five key routes have been identified in the pursuit of attaining your dream. The first is the formal or traditional path where you work in a formal setting and progress to the top. The second is hybrid route where you work in the formal (along the traditional) setting until such a time that you are confident of your abilities to survive on your own. At this point, you branch to set up on your own using the alternative path. The third is the alternative route. With this model, you would find it impossible to rise through the formal route. So what you do is to chart your own course. There is a fourth, which is quasi- alternative route. The last route is the one, neither by hard work nor networking but by 'favour'. It is rare, but cannot be ignored. It is misleading yet cannot be overlooked. Some people, out of nowhere, are too blessed to be ignored by good fate and favour.

The Formal or Traditional Route

The formal route is designed for corporate or organizational world where structure has been established. It has conventions and established ways of doing business or promotions or otherwise. Anyone within its fold goes through the structure. It is a rigid structure, designed and cast without flexibility. Migration to the next levels is normally by promotion which is based on predetermined criteria.

Basically you migrate from class one to two to three and so forth. For instance, you would have a junior manager moving to the senior management position and so forth till he is appointed chief executive.

In Prose

It was the dream of Kumi Boakye to be the Manager of Assante, an IT company, the very day he received his appointment letter as an assistant programmer in 1987. He has a degree in Computer Programming from IPMC, Ghana.

Kumi Boakye was young and ambitious. He was hardworking, a team worker, a good learner and honest. Indeed, he possessed the necessary values and cultivated them. He undertook certificate courses along the way, attended seminars and built a strong network within Assante and beyond. Gradually, he worked his way up the company. At the early stages, he was assigned to work on Assante's projects with the government of Dubai and other leading banks and industries in the West African hub.

In his seventh year, he was promoted to senior programmer, reporting directly to the Vice President responsible for International Projects.

In his ninth year, having proven himself as an innovator and trustworthy, he was promoted again as the deputy to the vice president for International Projects with a team of twelve senior developers working under him. It is worth stating that, Kumi's rise was characterised by hard work, dedication, and self belief. He was an innovator and was not afraid to think outside the box. He was a fast learner and learned to make himself useful to many of his bosses.

Kumi's rise was not smooth though. In a year after his promotion to Senior Programmes Manager, he was suspended, after lengthy investigations, for losing a company laptop containing new billing software for online retail giant Safera. The loss of the laptop and the subsequent piracy of the software was a major blow to the company because it cost them their contract with Safera. He was punished. For seven (7) months he remained holed at home.

With his record under suspicion, he could not look for another job. These were difficult months for Kumi. He suffered serious emotional trauma, depression and crisis of confidence and self belief. He lost many friends, the love of his wife and her touch. It was a low end of his life. Several times he asked himself; 'what did I do wrong?' and wondered if there would ever be better days ahead. During these low times, he learnt much of what many books could not teach him: the art of life; the cold grinding wheel of reality; the ups and downs of life and their corresponding whips.

Most importantly, he learnt attitudes of friends and colleagues at this time of his life. People who had hailed him as the future of Assante now turned him down, even for a visit. People he commanded at his department now refused to return his call or even reply to his mails.

He was eventually cleared after a six-month investigation. Kumi was not reinstated to his former position though. Rather, he was demoted to serve as a programmer reporting to his former junior. With no immediate offers from rival firms, he hanged on. His talents were not diminished. He found his balance and touch and began to rise again. This time more carefully.

Three years after his reinstatement, he resigned to take up new challenges at a rival firm, Afyna, a Social Network giant for professionals. After ten years at Afyna, Kumi retired at the age of fifty-five (55) to enjoy happy days with his family. He was the President for Projects Development at the time of his retirement.

Within his nearly thirty-year career span, he saw failures, setbacks, doubts, rebukes and disappointments and happy moments. Kumi sought to achieve his dream of becoming the President and he did. He achieved through the channels laid down by the companies he worked for. He was a career oriented professional.

Conditions for the traditional route

1. When your career aspiration lies in administration or the corporate world

2. If you are a team player

3. Availability of job opportunity

Advantages

1. There is an established structure with less likelihood of collapse.

2. You have a secured source of income and livelihood.

3. There are large pools of mentors, role models and lessons to learn.

4. Less risky in term of income. Thus, it provides you with job security.

5. It gives you space and room to take a long-term view of your aspirations.

6. It is the best grounds for learning the basics of your profession.

7. It gives you ample room for understanding the human character which a thousand management and psychology books shall not be able to imbue.

8. It gives you time to create, reassess and formulate your career.

9. It provides a platform for building a lasting network with the highest levels and best minds in your profession.

10. It gives you an overall perspective on organizational culture without which you may not succeed on your own.

Challenges

1. Too structured to allow for innovation.

2. Not suited for radical ideas.

3. Takes too much time to grow to the top.

4. People in the structure are burdened with unnecessary bureaucracy and traditions.

5. You sometimes spend more time infighting than in achieving your dreams.

6. You are sometimes compelled to sacrifice creativity for the sake of preserving traditions.

7. It kills confidence of young minds.

8. It sometimes makes you docile and you may lack initiative.

9. It makes you risk averse, thereby becoming too cautious.

The Alternative Route

The second identified route is the alternative route. This is a fundamental route ignoring the lengthy stretch of the traditional route. Some visions are novelty. Others have huge stumbling blocks within the traditional environment. Such dreams require that the youth take a measured risk to embark on their dreams through their own created paths. It is to say that when you see no road ahead for your dreams, you create your own path. For example; Steve Jobs (Apple); Bill Gates (Microsoft); Larry Page and Sergey Brin (Google); and Jerry Yang and David Filo (Yahoo) all created their own paths to achieving their dreams. There are other countless examples outside IT.

It is worth noting that, the alternative route is a means where pioneers, pathfinders and leaders create and invent new ways of doing things. It is an avenue where outside-the-box thinkers and innovators strive to create new worlds and dimensions. It is a route for pathfinders.

Conditions necessitating the Alternative Route

1.   When there is no precedent to what is to be done.

2.   When the status quo does not allow the new ideas or dreams to be nurtured and realised.

3.   When the cost of creating a new and independent route is less than the cost of fighting the status quo.

4.   When it is less risky to create your own business growth strategies, growth paths, assessment methods, financing models, management structure and related issues relative to your business.

5.   In a situation when the business is to operate in a fast paced environment requiring quick decision making.

Advantages of Using the Alternative-Route

1.   It frees you from the difficulties of dealing with entrenched positions within the industry you wish to operate in.

2.   It enables you to create routes that suit your particular growth plans.

3.   It enables you to control the stages in your career growth and /or business operations.

4.   It shields the business from pitfalls of the traditional route.

5. The alternative route method provides protection for new entrants.

Challenges

1. It is tedious to create new routes.

2. It takes a long time to identify the best route to create and choose.

3. It faces strong opposition from the status quo. This could result in a protracted struggle.

4. It could be financially expensive.

5. It has the potential for confusing the young entrepreneur.

The Hybrid Route

The hybrid route is a combination of the Traditional Route and Alternative Route. You start with the traditional and at a point when enough skills and financial capital have been raised, you break away to pursue your dreams on your own path along the alternative route. The central theme of this route is further skills acquisition and capital. The basic knowledge gained by way of education or initial skills are really not enough. So you bid your time along the traditional route, gain more knowledge, build effective networks, and the financial capital needed to start up.

Conditions necessitating the Hybrid Route

1. When you have ample time to start your dream venture.

2. When you have a godfather-like figure to look up to.

3. When your venture needs continuous skills, well above what you can give.

4. When the venture requires the support of old friends in former business arena, as per marketing, clientele (local and international) and goodwill.

5. When in the dream quest, you have partnership support from people within or outside your former business domain

6. When you deem correctly that you need 'protection'.

Advantages

1. It has low risks.
2. It is flexible.
3. It allows for realignment with other methods.
4. It allows for gradual set up and as a result does not put pressure on you to raise huge initial start up costs.
5. It has high success rate.

Challenges

1. It takes longer years to start.
2. It is idealistic.
3. It is expensive.

The Quasi-Alternative Route

The fourth route is the quasi-alternative route. Here, from the growth platform, you make a decision to pursue your dreams along the alternative route until you identify an opening on the traditional path. When you decide to hop onto the traditional route, you usually get a head start over your colleagues who might have started fresh on the traditional route. There are two classes though. There are those of you who genuinely set out to go on the alternative route but branch off when they see an opening in the traditional route. For instance, the person starts a professional life as a self-employed salesman, but at a point he abandons his job and takes up employment as a salesman with another institution.

On the other hand, there are those of you whose sole aim on the alternative route was not by choice but by circumstance. For example in the 1990's, many students went to Teacher Training College because they could not gain admission to sixth form. As soon as they re-sat their papers and improved their grades, they quit the Training Colleges for sixth form to prepare for direct entry into universities.

On this route, an experience in a particular field would be transferred onto a related field. It does not necessarily mean migrating onto the traditional field on the same field or profession as you were. For instance, a pop star could use her name, recognition, and network to enter the movie industry. So could a television hostess secure a second profession in the movie or music industry. A particular notice is that, when they do migrate, you do not start from scratch as you would have been if you had gone by the traditional route. Rather, you start at a higher level.

The Achievement Platform

The last realistic stage is the achievement platform. This is the period of rest. It signifies achievement, experience, wisdom and conclusion. There is no room for redress at this stage. You have reached here having achieved your dreams or having missed opportunities. But this stage is specifically for those who have reached the end of the line, having achieved their dreams to the fullest or have their dreams truncated by the harsh realities of life, and have no more strength left to fight on.

This is the stage where dreams become reality or otherwise. This is an important but less fully achieved stage. This stage has three levels. These are the stress rest, contentment and fulfilment levels.

The last stage is the time you say to yourself, 'I am at home'. When you say, 'this is it'. 'I have lived my life to the fullest or my best'. This is the last stop when you wish to go no further. This is the period when the pleasures of life, the furies of ambition, the struggles of dreams and ego look meaningless to you. You see young executives, employees and entrepreneurs struggle to rise and you shake your head and laugh away. You have seen it all. You have been here before. It is more idealistic to say someone would have achieved his dream to the fullest. It would be difficult to achieve the mystic dream. What is promoted here is the dream achieved in the spirit of contentment.

The stress rest level is the type of achievement when you reach and say, 'this is not enough', but you are bound by time to accept this achievement. The achievements are modest. You are not content with them but there is not much you can do.

Time has run out for you and as such, you have decided to accept whatever of your dreams have been achieved. You see it as not enough but you are at the end. You have the energy, motivation and drive to go on but circumstances have prevailed upon you to retire. You are bitter, angry and restless but there is nothing to do than to retire and mentally retrace your footsteps. This terminal stage could be brought about by age (as in the case of public sector workers who have compulsory retirement age), ill-health or any misfortune beyond your control.

The contentment level is the dream achievement. Those who achieve this state are said to have achieved their vision. It is not the perfect dreams they had years back and worked for. What they have achieved is near it. They are content. Their strength is gone and there is not much to do. They have achieved more than the stress rest. You have achieved something you feel you could be proud of; something worth talking about to your grandchildren. You have no regrets. You have peace in your heart. After all, you set out to reach level seven (7) and you reached five (5). You had dreams to conquer the world. At the end of your life, you managed to conquer Africa, Asia and South America. It is okay for you.

The fulfilment level is the fullness level; the ultimate achievement. You have achieved everything you set your heart and mind to achieve. You have achieved and lived the dream with peace and happiness in your heart and mind. On this level, you go all the way up to the top. It is like a Member of Parliament becoming the President of his country; an accounts clerk becoming the Chief Accountant; a Junior Manager becoming the Chief Executive Officer; a police Sergeant rising to become the Inspector General or Commissioner of Police.

One critical element of this stage is that, those who have achieved it have done so and lived in peace and harmony with their conscience. There is no fear of afterthought haunting them. They have peace with themselves, their society and with God, their Creator.

If a policeman dreams to rise to become Deputy Inspector General, and he achieves it, that is his fulfilment. If a lecturer dreams of rising to Associate Professor and he reaches that level, that is his fulfilment.

The 'Dream' Stage

This period is beyond the fulfillment level. You have gone beyond fulfilment and you are at a level you never knew of, never dreamt of and so did not wish for. This is the final dream. The subconscious dreams of a child at seven has been realised and gone beyond. The pure dreams of childhood have survived the turmoil of this life to come face to face with reality and have conquered. Those who reach this stage usually say, 'I never thought I would be here'. 'This is more than I asked for'. It is a time of bliss and humility.

At this level, you have no care for money, fame, or power. You are above the pull and tug of the flesh. You have come to see the fruitlessness of money, temporal power and self-seeking ambitions. You are in the circle of Noblemen. You have become a watcher of the affairs of men, laughing at the needless squabbles of men struggling to rise and conquer the world.

You have become an encyclopaedia of wisdom and knowledge. You are a prophet. You could look at a person and tell where the path he has taken would end. You have become a form of a god.

The Four Arcs

Beyond The Dream level are four arcs. The first arc is the geographic level. The second is the territorial level; the third, universal level and the fourth, mystic level. Each of these arcs is a level of greatness. There is no doubt that Frederick Carlton; Kofi Annan; Nelson Mandela, George Oppong Weah, Kwame Nkrumah and Mohandas Karamchand Gandhi are all great men.

The Geographic Level

Those who are on the Geographic Level are the ones who fulfilled their lives within a geographic area, say a city or a nation. Their fulfilment is what they dreamt to achieve within the walls of their cities or nation. Once that is done, their dreams were achieved. They become watchers of the affairs of that state. They lived and were fulfilled in a particular geographic area. It could be a nation or a sub-region. They are national champions. They become legends in their societies or nations.

The Territorial Level

The Territorial Level is achieved by people in a professional setting. Men of this category achieve their watcher status in a particular profession, say in Soccer, Chemistry, Music or Business. They are world icons since their professions are practiced world-wide. Beyond their professions, they may be relatively unknown or less considered.

They are national as well as world icons in their areas of trade. Men like Pele for Soccer, Albert Einstein for Physics, George Washington for Governance and Politics, and Nasta 'Bob' Marley for Reggae Music are a few examples. With time, they easily migrate into the Universal level as they take roles beyond their traditional trades. For instance, Edison "Edson" Arantes do Nascimento (Pele) is for soccer but his recent pro-poor programmes using soccer has earned him acclaim and recognition beyond soccer.

The Universal Level

The third, the Universal Level, is achieving world recognition beyond two territorial areas. Their achievements were fulfilled and accepted as influencing many areas of endeavours worldwide. Men like Sir Isaac Newton, Socrates, Leonardo da Vinci and Nelson Mandela are Universal Level achievers. They are revered and adored for their greatness not on the basis of a particular field of endeavour, but because of an aura around them which influences life on many fronts.

The Mystic Level

The final arc is the Mystic Level. These are gods of our universe. Their achievements are regarded as groundbreaking, unprecedented, revered and worshipped. They transcend race, colour and profession. They travel timelessly in time. In simple language, they pull humanity to higher levels of spirituality and shed new light to humanity. They are rare and few. Their abilities are beyond human imaginations. They are the gods among men or lived among men. In life or death, they have the power to influence the affairs of men with words, the silence of their absence or their names.

Their names have come to stand for certain good values or cause able to direct and enhance human endeavours. Among these gods are Jesus Christ, the son of Joseph and Mary; The Buddha, Prophet Mohammed, Krishna and Moses.

THE END

Africa, Dream Again!

Africa, Dream Beyond the Stars!

AU ANTHEM

Let us all unite and celebrate together
The victories won for our liberation;
Let us dedicate ourselves to rise together
To defend our liberty and unity.

O Sons and Daughters of Africa,
Flesh of the Sun and Flesh of the Sky;
Let us make Africa the Tree of Life.

Let us all unite and sing together
To uphold the bond that frames our destiny;
Let us dedicate ourselves to fight together
For lasting peace and justice on earth.

O Sons and Daughters of Africa,
Flesh of the Sun and Flesh of the Sky;
Let us make Africa the Tree of Life.

Let us all unite and toil together
To give the best we have to Africa;
The cradle of mankind and fount of culture,
Our pride and hope at break of dawn.

O Sons and Daughters of Africa,
Flesh of the Sun and Flesh of the Sky;
Let us make Africa the Tree of Life.

(This should not be an anthem for euphoria; rather, it should be a benchmark to hold the African leadership to account. Take note of these words and phrases: unity, justice, peace, dedicate ourselves, toil together, sing together, rise together, and give our best to Africa, (we)the cradle of mankind and fountain of culture)

Let the African Youth Dream again, because a Great future lies ahead...

Index